"A book that displays the impressive breadth of Lewis's appeal across denominational boundaries and that helpfully highlights the continuing importance of his example as a Christian who could think both rationally and imaginatively. Altogether an interesting, lively, and thought-provoking read."

Michael Ward, Fellow of Blackfriars Hall, University of Oxford; author, *Planet Narnia: The Seven Heavens in the Imagination of C. S. Lewis*

"For many of us, the writings of C. S. Lewis have been a helpful guide to the nooks and crannies of the Christian life. As noted by a number of the authors of this extremely helpful collection of essays, the rich coloring of all of Lewis's work has been a tonic in the gray drabness of contemporary life. Although none of the authors would endorse every element of Lewis's thinking, each is well aware that to neglect Lewis is to miss out on one of God's surprising gifts in the twentieth century. A great introduction to and reflection on a remarkable Christian!"

Michael A. G. Haykin, Professor of Church History and Biblical Spirituality, The Southern Baptist Theological Seminary

"Paints a well-rounded, sharply observed portrait that balances criticism with a deep love and appreciation for the works and witness of Lewis. The writers have all absorbed Lewis into their bones, and they invite us to do the same."

Louis Markos, Professor in English, Scholar in Residence, and Robert H. Ray Chair in Humanities, Houston Baptist University; author, *Restoring Beauty: The Good, the True, and the Beautiful in the Writings of C. S. Lewis*

"A warm-hearted, engaging, and thoroughly thought-out appreciation of evangelicalism's enormous debt to C. S. Lewis that also looks squarely at differences, real and imagined. With well-chosen and varied contributors, it presents a deep understanding and wide reading of Lewis and also reaches toward the secret of Lewis's profound and health-giving influence on Christianity throughout the world."

Colin Duriez, author, *Tolkien and C. S. Lewis: The Gift of Friendship; A-Z of C. S. Lewis;* and *J. R. R. Tolkien: The Making of a Legend*

"In order to explore the world that is Lewis, we need faithful guides, explorers who have charted his terrain, both the familiar and the back roads where few have dared to tread. The authors have not just looked at Lewis, as though he were some theological or literary curiosity; they've looked along Lewis, laboring to see with the freshness of his vision, and then draw us further up and further in so that we too come to see the real world, and God, and Christ, with new eyes."

Joe Rigney, Assistant Professor of Theology and Christian Worldview, Bethlehem College and Seminary; author, *Live Like a Narnian: Christian Discipleship in Lewis's Chronicles*

"Lewis fans of all persuasions will enjoy this collection of essays. More than just a celebration of Lewis, the authors celebrate what Lewis celebrated and point to the one he pointed to. The authors don't always agree with Lewis (itself a good and healthy thing), but they always understand and appreciate him and help us to do so as well. Most of all, in these essays they share Lewis's ultimate goal—that of kindling and nurturing a desire for God."

Devin Brown, author, *A Life Observed: A Spiritual Biography of C. S. Lewis*

THE ROMANTIC RATIONALIST

Other Desiring God conference books

Acting the Miracle: God's Work and Ours in the Mystery of Sanctification, 2013

Finish the Mission: Bringing the Gospel to the Unreached and Unengaged, 2012

Thinking. Loving. Doing.: A Call to Glorify God with Heart and Mind, 2011

With Calvin in the Theater of God: The Glory of Christ and Everyday Life, 2010

The Power of Words and the Wonder of God, 2009

Stand: A Call for the Endurance of the Saints, 2008

The Supremacy of Christ in a Postmodern World, 2007

Suffering and the Sovereignty of God, 2006

Sex and the Supremacy of Christ, 2005

A God-Entranced Vision of All Things: The Legacy of Jonathan Edwards, 2004

THE ROMANTIC RATIONALIST

God, Life, and Imagination in the Work of C. S. Lewis

EDITED BY

JOHN PIPER & DAVID MATHIS

WITH CONTRIBUTIONS FROM

Randy Alcorn, Philip Ryken, Kevin Vanhoozer, and Douglas Wilson

CROSSWAY

WHEATON, ILLINOIS

Library of Congress Cataloging-in-Publication Data

The romantic rationalist : God, life, and imagination in the work of C.S. Lewis / edited by David Mathis and John Piper ; with contributions from Randy Alcorn, Philip Ryken, Kevin Vanhoozer, and Douglas Wilson.
    pages cm
  Includes bibliographical references and index.
  ISBN 978-1-4335-4498-9 (tp)
  1. Lewis, C. S. (Clive Staples), 1898–1963. I. Mathis, David, 1980– editor.
BX4827.L44R65   2014
230.092—dc23   2014010881

Crossway is a publishing ministry of Good News Publishers.

VP		24	23	22	21	20	19	18	17	16	15	14
15	14	13	12	11	10	9	8	7	6	5	4	3	2	1

To Campus Outreach
and its partnering churches,
students, staff, alumni, and supporters,
building laborers on the college campus
for the lost world
to the glory of God

CONTENTS

CONTRIBUTORS

Randy Alcorn is author of more than forty books, including bestsellers *Heaven*; *The Treasure Principle*; and *Safely Home*. He served as a pastor for almost fifteen years and is founder and director of Eternal Perspective Ministries. Randy and his wife, Nanci, have two daughters and five grandsons.

David Mathis is executive editor at desiringGod.org, elder at Bethlehem Baptist Church (Minneapolis, Minnesota), and adjunct professor at Bethlehem College and Seminary (Minneapolis). He writes regularly at desiringGod.org and is coauthor of *How to Stay Christian in Seminary* (2014), and coeditor of *Acting the Miracle* (2013); *Finish the Mission* (2012); *Thinking. Loving. Doing.* (2011); and *With Calvin in the Theater of God* (2010). David and his wife, Megan, have three children.

John Piper is founder and teacher of desiringGod.org and chancellor of Bethlehem College and Seminary. For thirty-three years, he was pastor at Bethlehem Baptist Church. He is author of more than fifty books, including *Desiring God*; *The Pleasures of God*; *Don't Waste Your Life*; and *Seeing and Savoring Jesus Christ*. John and his wife, Noël, have five children and twelve grandchildren.

Philip Ryken is eighth president of Wheaton College (Wheaton, Illinois). For fifteen years he served as senior minister at Tenth Presbyterian Church (Philadelphia). He studied at Wheaton (undergraduate); Westminster (MDiv); and Oxford (PhD) and is author of *Loving the Way Jesus Loves* (2012) and more than forty Bible commentaries and other books. He and his wife, Lisa, have five children.

Kevin Vanhoozer is research professor of systematic theology at Trinity Evangelical Divinity School (Deerfield, Illinois). He is author of *Is There Meaning in This Text?* (1998) and *The Drama of Doctrine: A Canonical-Linguistic Approach to Christian Theology* (2006), among other books. He studied at Westminster (MDiv) and Cambridge (PhD), and is also an amateur classical pianist. He is married to Sylvie, and they have two daughters.

Douglas Wilson is pastor of Christ Church (Moscow, Idaho). He is a founding board member of Logos School, instructor at Greyfriars Hall, and editor of *Credenda Agenda*. He is the author of many books, including *Father Hunger: Why God Calls Men to Love and Lead Their Families* (2013); *Wordsmithy: Hot Tips for the Writing Life* (2011); and *What I Learned in Narnia* (2010). He is married to Nancy and a father of three.

INTRODUCTION

Half a Century since C. S. Lewis

DAVID MATHIS

He went quietly. It was very British.

While the Americans rocked and reeled, and the world's attention turned to Dallas and the assassination of President John F. Kennedy, one Clive Staples Lewis breathed his last in Oxford just a week shy of his sixty-fifth birthday. Strangely enough, science-fictionist Aldous Huxley passed the same day, and in one calendar square, three of the twentieth century's most influential figures were gone.

It was November 22, 1963—now more than fifty years ago.

C. S. Lewis is known best for his series of seven short fiction books, the Chronicles of Narnia, which have sold over 100 million copies in forty languages. With three of the stories already becoming major motion pictures, and the fourth in the making, Lewis is as popular today as he's ever been. But even before he published Narnia in the early 1950s, he distinguished himself as a professor at Oxford and Cambridge, the world's foremost expert in medieval and Renaissance English literature, and as one of the great lay thinkers and writers in two millennia of the Christian church.

Discovering Truth and Joy

Good Brit though he was, Lewis was Irish, born in Belfast in 1898. He became an atheist in his teens and stridently such in his twenties, before slowly warming to theism in his early thirties, and finally being fully converted to Christianity at age thirty-three. And he would prove to be for many, as he was for his friend Owen Barfield, the "most thoroughly converted man I ever met."

What catches the eye about Lewis's star in the constellation of Christian thinkers and writers is his utter commitment to both the life of the mind and the life of the heart. He thinks and feels with the best. Lewis insisted that rigorous thought and deep affection were not at odds but mutually supportive. And as impressive as he was in arguing for it, he was even more convincing in his demonstration.

What eventually led Lewis to theism, and finally to Christianity, was what he called "Longing"—an ache for Joy with a capital J. He had learned all too well that relentless rationality could not adequately explain the depth and complexity of human life or the textures and hues of the world in which we find ourselves. From early on, an angst gnawed at him, which one day he would express so memorably in his most well-known single book, *Mere Christianity*: "If I find in myself a desire which no experience in this world can satisfy, the most probable explanation is that I was made for another world."[1]

This World and the Other

Such is the heart of his genius, his spiritual genius. So few treat the world in all its detail and contour like he does, and yet so few tirelessly point us beyond this world, with all its concreteness and color and taste, with the aggression and ardor of C. S. Lewis.

And so for many, his impact has been so personal. For me, it was a six-word sentence in Lewis—"We are far too easily pleased"—that popped the hood on a massive remodeling of my soul:

> If we consider the unblushing promises of reward and the staggering nature of the rewards promised in the Gospels, it would seem that Our Lord finds our desires not too strong, but too weak. We are half-hearted creatures, fooling about with drink and sex

<hr>

[1] C. S. Lewis, *Mere Christianity* (San Francisco: HarperCollins, 2001), 136–37.

and ambition when infinite joy is offered us, like an ignorant child who wants to go on making mud pies in a slum because he cannot imagine what is meant by the offer of a holiday at the sea. *We are far too easily pleased.*[2]

Does Jesus really find our desires not too strong but too weak? I had long professed Christianity, but this tasted so different from what I knew. It tasted! This affirmation of happiness and pleasure and desire and delight was, to me, so new in the context of the Christian faith. And Lewis was the chef.

My notions about God and the Christian life were exposed as mere duty driven, and my soul was thrilling at the possibility that Christianity might not mean muting my desires but being encouraged (even commanded!) to turn them up—up to God.

The Language of Hedonism Everywhere

Lewis was conspiring with others to help open my mind and heart to a new angle on God and life—that new angle being joy and delight—but my upbringing determined that there must be a final and decisive test for this freshman discovery: *Will this hold in the Scriptures?* I thank God my parents and home church had so clearly taught me that the Bible is trustworthy and inerrant and the final authority on every seemingly true line of thinking.

And with Bible open, it didn't take long. Equipped with this new lens—the spectacles of joy—the Scriptures began popping like never before. Lewis's hedonism was confirmed on page after page.

In God's presence, says Psalm 16:11, "there is fullness of joy; at [his] right hand are pleasures forevermore." I had no category for that until then. Or for the heart cry of Psalm 63:1: "O God, you are my God; earnestly I seek you; my soul thirsts for you; my flesh faints for you, as in a dry and weary land where there is no water." Or for the holy longing of Psalm 42:1–2: "As a deer pants for flowing streams,

---

[2] C. S. Lewis, *The Weight of Glory* (New York: HarperOne, 2009), 26 (emphasis added).

so pants my soul for you, O God. My soul thirsts for God, for the living God." As John Piper says, after Lewis helped open his eyes, "I turned to the Psalms for myself and found the language of Hedonism everywhere."[3]

At last I was ready to hear Paul say, "Rejoice in the Lord" (Phil. 3:1). And the reprise: "Rejoice in the Lord always; again I will say, rejoice" (Phil. 4:4). And Jesus: "The kingdom of heaven is like treasure hidden in a field, which a man found and covered up. Then *in his joy* he goes and sells all that he has and buys that field" (Matt. 13:44). As well as the glimpse we're given into his very heart at the heart of our faith: "For the joy that was set before him [he] endured the cross" (Heb. 12:2). And on and on.

Lewis's help, just at this one point, has been invaluable.

Feel the Weight of Glory

And there's even a little bit more to squeeze from the six-word sentence. Lewis would say that not only are we "far too easily pleased" when we settle for fixing our soul's inconsolable longing on anything other than God, but also that we're too easily pleased if we see God only from a distance and not soon be drawn into him. This, says Lewis, is "the weight of glory." As a layman, Lewis didn't preach weekly but occasionally had his chance at a pulpit. His most remembered sermon is one he preached under this title—"The Weight of Glory."

> The promise of glory is the promise, almost incredible and only possible by the work of Christ, that some of us, that any of us who really chooses, shall actually survive that examination [of standing before God], shall find approval, shall please God. To please God . . . to be a real ingredient in the divine happiness . . . to be loved by God, not merely pitied, but delighted in as an artist delights in his work or a father in a son—it seems impossible, a

[3] John Piper, *Desiring God: Meditations of a Christian Hedonist* (Colorado Springs, CO: Multnomah, 2011), 23.

weight or burden of glory which our thoughts can hardly sustain. But so it is.[4]

Indeed, we are far too easily pleased when we pine finally for anything less than God—and when we ache only for seeing his splendor from afar, rather than going further up and further in, to being "accepted, welcomed, or taken into the dance."[5] The weight of glory "means good report with God, acceptance by God, response, acknowledgement, and welcome into the heart of things."[6]

Our Creator has written on our hearts not only to enjoy eternity as a spectator in his majestic stadium, watching happily from the bleachers, but also, being brought onto the field, given a jersey, and adopted as a full member of his team, to live in his acceptance and embrace. We never become God, but we do become spectacularly one with him in his Son and our glad conformity to Jesus (Rom. 8:29). Surely such is a weight of glory almost too great to even consider in our current condition.

No Ordinary People

When Lewis breathed his last and quietly slipped from this life, more than half a century ago now, he took one big step toward becoming the kind of glorious creature in the coming new creation that he speaks about in that sermon:

> It is a serious thing to live in a society of possible gods and goddesses, to remember that the dullest and most uninteresting person you can talk to may one day be a creature which, if you saw it now, you would be strongly tempted to worship, or else a horror and a corruption such as you now meet, if at all, only in a nightmare.
>
> All day long we are, in some degree, helping each other to one or other of these destinations. It is in the light of these over-

---

[4] Lewis, *Weight of Glory*, 38–39.
[5] Ibid., 40.
[6] Ibid., 41.

whelming possibilities, it is with the awe and the circumspection proper to them, that we should conduct all our dealings with one another, all friendships, all loves, all play, all politics.

There are no ordinary people. You have never talked to a mere mortal. Nations, cultures, arts, civilisations—these are mortal, and their life is to ours as the life of a gnat. But it is immortals whom we joke with, work with, marry, snub, and exploit—immortal horrors or everlasting splendours.

This does not mean that we are to be perpetually solemn. We must play. But our merriment must be of that kind (and it is, in fact, the merriest kind) which exists between people who have, from the outset, taken each other seriously.[7]

For a growing number of us, Lewis occupies a class to himself. Few, if any, have taught us so much about this world, and the next, save the Scriptures.

The Romantic Rationalist

Perhaps that's why you've turned to this book. We hope you've dipped into Lewis for yourself, whether his *Mere Christianity*; *The Screwtape Letters*; *The Abolition of Man*; the Chronicles of Narnia; or his voluminous, brilliant, personal correspondence. You know that his writings are pervasively thoughtful, engaging, provoking, and rewarding and that he only rarely disappoints. And now you want more.

More than any other, chapter 1 addresses Lewis, the man. John Piper explains why it is that we join Peter Kreeft in calling Lewis a "romantic rationalist." Chapters 2 and 3 then tackle two of the larger concerns Reformed evangelicals raise about Lewis's theology: his doctrine of Scripture (especially inerrancy) and his doctrine of salvation. Philip Ryken and Douglas Wilson, respectively, tackle these two tough issues with brilliance and flair.

Next Kevin Vanhoozer turns to Lewis's vision of the imagina-

---

[7] C. S. Lewis, *The Weight of Glory and Other Addresses* (New York: HarperOne, 1949), 45–46.

tion, its relevance, and even essentiality, for Christian doctrine and discipleship. Then Randy Alcorn brings us soaring with Lewis into the new heavens and the new earth. Finally, Piper rounds out our study with an exposition of the very "Lewisian" text 1 Timothy 4:1–5 and what we can glean from the apostle Paul and the Oxford don. (Appendix 1 is Alcorn's treatment of Lewis's controversial take on the doctrine of hell, and appendix 2 is a lightly edited conversation among the contributors.)

We wouldn't want this book to keep you from reading Lewis yourself, but we hope that these reflections on his work and vision of the world will deepen not only your appreciation of Lewis but, even more, of his Lord.

1

C. S. LEWIS, ROMANTIC RATIONALIST

How His Paths to Christ Shaped His Life and Ministry

JOHN PIPER

For those of you who may wonder why we would devote a book to a mere mortal like C. S. Lewis, let's begin with an accolade from Peter Kreeft from a book chapter titled, "The Romantic Rationalist: Lewis the Man."

> Once upon a dreary era, when the world of . . . specialization had nearly made obsolete all universal geniuses, romantic poets, Platonic idealists, rhetorical craftsmen, and even orthodox Christians, there appeared a man (almost as if from another world, one of the worlds of his own fiction: was he a man or something more like elf or Angel?) who was all of these things as amateur, as well as probably the world's foremost authority in his professional province, Medieval and Renaissance English literature. Before his death in 1963 he found time to produce some first-quality works of literary history, literary criticism, theology, philosophy, autobiography, biblical studies, historical philology, fantasy, science fiction, letters, poems, sermons, formal and informal essays, a historical novel, a spiritual diary, religious allegory, short stories,

and children's novels. Clive Staples Lewis was not a man: he was a world.[1]

Those are the kinds of accolades you read again and again. Which means there must have been something extraordinary about the man. Indeed, we believe there was. And in this fiftieth year since his death, it seemed to many of us that a book like this would be a small expression of our thankfulness to God for him, and our admiration of him, and our desire that his gifts to the world be preserved and spread.

Childhood and Schooling

The various authors in this book draw out facts of Lewis's life that are relevant to their concern, but let me give you a three-minute summary of his life so that some of the hard facts are before us. Lewis loved hard facts. The kind you want under your house when the rains come down and the floods come up.

Lewis was born in 1898 in Belfast, Ireland. His mother died when he was nine years old, and his father never remarried. Between the death of his mother in August 1908 and the autumn of 1914, Lewis attended four different boarding schools. Then for two and a half years, he studied with William Kirkpatrick, whom he called the Great Knock. And there his emerging atheism was confirmed, and his reasoning powers were refined in an extraordinary way. Lewis said, "If ever a man came near to being a purely logical entity that man was Kirk."[2] He described himself later as a seventeen-year-old rationalist.

Becoming the Voice

But just as his rationalism was at its peak, he stumbled onto George MacDonald's fantasy novel *Phantastes*. "That night," he said, "my

[1] Peter Kreeft, *C. S. Lewis: A Critical Essay* (Grand Rapids, MI: Eerdmans, 1969), 4.
[2] C. S. Lewis, *Surprised by Joy: The Shape of My Early Life* (New York: Harcourt, Brace, & World, 1955), 135.

imagination was, in a certain sense, baptized."[3] Something had broken in—a "new quality," a "bright shadow," he called it.[4] The romantic impulse of his childhood was again awake. Only now it seemed real, and holy.

At eighteen, he took his place at Oxford University, but before he could begin his studies, he entered the army, and in February of 1918 he was wounded in France and returned to England to recover. He resumed his studies in Oxford in January 1919 and over the next six years took three first-class honors in classics, humanities, and English literature. He became a teaching fellow in October 1925 at the age of twenty-six.

Six years later, in 1931, he professed faith in Jesus Christ and was settled in the conviction that Christianity is true. Within ten years he had become the "voice of faith" for the nation of England during the Second World War, and his broadcast talks in 1941–1942 "achieved classic status."[5]

Lewis in Full Flower

He was now in the full flower of his creative and apologetic productivity. In his prime, he was probably the world's leading authority on medieval English Literature and, according to one of his adversaries, "the best read man of his generation."[6] But he was vastly more. Books of many kinds were rolling out: *The Pilgrim's Regress*; *The Allegory of Love*; *The Screwtape Letters*; *Perelandra*. Then in 1950 began the Chronicles of Narnia. All these titles were of different genres and showed the amazing versatility of Lewis as a writer and thinker and imaginative visionary.

He appeared on the cover of *Time* magazine in 1947. Then, after thirty years at Oxford, he took a professorship in Medieval and Renaissance English at the University of Cambridge in 1955. The next

---

[3] Ibid., 181.
[4] Ibid., 179.
[5] Alister McGrath, *C. S. Lewis: Eccentric Genius, Reluctant Prophet* (Carol Stream, IL: Tyndale, 2013), 210.
[6] Ibid., 166.

year, at the age of fifty-seven, he married Joy Davidman. And just short of their fourth anniversary, she died of cancer, and three and a half years later—two weeks short of his sixty-fifth birthday, on November 22, 1963—Lewis followed her in death.

A Life of Pointing

Lewis is more popular as an author today than at any time during his life. The Chronicles of Narnia alone have gone on to sell over 100 million copies in forty languages.[7] One of the reasons for this appeal, I am going to argue, is that Lewis is a romantic rationalist to an exceptionally high and healthy degree.

My thesis is that his romanticism and his rationalism were the paths on which he came to Christ, and they are the paths on which he lived his life and did his work. They shaped him into a teacher and writer with extraordinary gifts for logic and likening. And with these gifts, he spent his life pointing people beyond the world to the meaning of the world, Jesus Christ.

The Romantic

So we will look first at his romanticism, and then at his rationality, and finally at the way they came together to lead him to Christ and to confirm the worldview where all of us are romantic rationalists in our truest humanity.

In August 1932, Lewis sat down and in fourteen days wrote his first novel, less than a year after professing faith in Christ.[8] *The Pilgrim's Regress* is a two-hundred-page allegory of his own pilgrimage to faith in Christ. The subtitle goes like this: "An Allegorical Apology for Christianity, Reason, and Romanticism." So he is defending being a romantic, a rationalist, and a Christian.

---

[7] http://ncronline.org/news/art-media/cs-lewis-couldnt-touch-anything-without-illuminating-it (accessed September 12, 2013).

[8] He wrote to his friend Arthur Greeves on October 1, 1931, "I have just passed on from believing in God to definitely believing in Christ—in Christianity." *The Collected Letters of C. S. Lewis, vol. 1: Family Letters 1905–1931*, ed. Walter Hooper (San Francisco: HarperSanFrancisco, 2004), 974.

Romanticism Means Joy

But ten years later, when the third edition of the book appeared, he added a ten-page preface to apologize for obscurity and to explain what he means by being a romantic. He said, "The cause for obscurity was the (unintentionally) 'private' meaning I then gave to the word 'Romanticism.'"[9] The word, as he used it, he said, described "the experience which is central in this book."

> What I meant by "Romanticism" . . . and what I would still be taken to mean on the title page of this book—was . . . a particular recurrent experience which dominated my childhood and adolescence and which I hastily called "Romantic" because inanimate nature and marvelous literature were among the things that evoked it.[10]

When we examine his description of the experience he refers to, it turns out to be identical with what ten years later in his autobiography he calls "Joy."[11]

> The experience [of romanticism] is one of intense longing. It is distinguished from other longings by two things. In the first place, though the sense of want is acute and even painful, yet the mere wanting is felt to be somehow a delight. . . . This hunger is better than any other fullness; this poverty better than all other wealth.[12]

> There is a peculiar mystery about the *object* of this Desire. Inexperienced people (and inattention leaves some inexperienced all their lives) suppose, when they feel it, that they know what they are desiring. [Some past event, some perilous ocean, some erotic

---

[9] C. S. Lewis, *The Pilgrim's Regress* (Grand Rapids, MI: Eerdmans, 1958), 5.
[10] Ibid., 7.
[11] In *Surprised by Joy*, pp. 17–18, Lewis said that this Joy is the experience "of an unsatisfied desire which is itself more desirable than any other satisfaction. . . . I call it Joy, which is here a technical term and must be sharply distinguished both from Happiness and from Pleasure. Joy (in my sense) has indeed one characteristic, and one only, in common with them; the fact that any one who has experienced it will want it again. Apart from that, and considered only in its quality, it might almost equally well be called a particular kind of unhappiness or grief. But then it is the kind we want. I doubt whether anyone who has tasted it would ever, if both were in his power, exchange it for all the pleasures in the world. But then Joy is never in our power and pleasure often is."
[12] Ibid.

suggestion, some beautiful meadow, some distant planet, some great achievement, some quest or great knowledge, etc.] . . .

But every one of these impressions is wrong. The sole merit I claim for this book is that it is written by one who has proved them all to be wrong. There is no room for vanity in the claim: I know them to be wrong not by intelligence but by experience. . . . For I have myself been deluded by every one of these false answers in turn, and have contemplated each of them earnestly enough to discover the cheat.[13]

If a man diligently followed this desire, pursuing the false objects until their falsity appeared and then resolutely abandoning them, he must come out at last into the clear knowledge that the human soul was made to enjoy some object that is never fully given—nay, cannot even be imagined as given—in our present mode of subjective and spatio-temporal existence.[14]

The Dialectic of Desire

Lewis called this experience a kind of lived ontological proof of God—or at least of something beyond the created world. "The dialectic of Desire," he said, "faithfully followed, would . . . force you not to propound, but to live through, a sort of ontological proof."[15]

Later, when he wrote *Mere Christianity*, he would state it most famously: "If I find in myself a desire which no experience in this world can satisfy, the most probable explanation is that I was made for another world."[16]

The Piercing Longing

So the essence of his romanticism is Lewis's experience of the world that repeatedly awakened in him a sense that there is always more than this created world—something other, something beyond the

---

13 Ibid., 8 (emphasis original).
14 Ibid., 10.
15 Ibid.
16 C. S. Lewis, *Mere Christianity* (New York: Macmillan, 1960), 106.

natural world. At first, he thought the stabbing desire and longing was what he really wanted. But after his conversion, he wrote, "I now know that the experience, considered as a state of my own mind, had never had the kind of importance I once gave it. It was valuable only as a pointer to something other and outer."[17]

And this other and outer—this more—was wonderful even before he knew that what he was longing for was God. And now that he was a Christian, the piercing longing did not go away just because he knew who it was: "I believe," he said, ". . . that the old stab, the old bittersweet, has come to me as often and as sharply since my conversion as at any time of my life."[18]

The Central Story of His Life

Alan Jacobs says, "Nothing was closer to the core of his being than this experience."[19] Clyde Kilby says, "In one way or other it hovers over nearly every one of his books."[20] And Lewis himself says, "In a sense the central story of my life is about nothing else."[21]

And when you read his repeated descriptions of this experience of romanticism or Joy in *Surprised by Joy* and *The Pilgrim's Regress* and *The Problem of Pain* and *The Weight of Glory*, you realize Lewis doesn't see this as a quirk of his personality but as a trait of humanness. All of us are romantics in this sense. Devin Brown says that Lewis's "use of the inclusive *you* in these passages . . . makes it clear that Lewis believes this is a longing we have all felt. . . . You might say this is the central story of everyone's life."[22]

Our Hidden Desire for Heaven

For example, in *The Problem of Pain*, Lewis makes the case that even people who think they have never desired heaven don't see things clearly:

---

[17] Lewis, *Surprised by Joy*, 238.

[18] Ibid.

[19] Alan Jacobs, *The Narnian: The Life and Imagination of C. S. Lewis* (New York: HarperOne, 2006), 42.

[20] Clyde S. Kilby, *The Christian World of C. S. Lewis* (Grand Rapids, MI: Eerdmans, 1964), 187.

[21] Lewis, *Surprised by Joy*, 17.

[22] Devin Brown, *A Life Observed: A Spiritual Biography of C. S. Lewis* (Grand Rapids, MI: Brazos, 2013), 5.

There have been times when I think we do not desire heaven, but more often I find myself wondering whether, in our heart of hearts, we have ever desired anything else . . . tantalizing glimpses, promises never quite fulfilled, echoes that died away just as they caught your ear. But if . . . there ever came an echo that did not die away, but swelled into the sound itself—you would know it. Beyond all possibility of doubt you would say, "here at last is the thing I was made for."[23]

So Lewis saw in his own experience of romanticism the universally human experience. We are all romantics. All of us experience from time to time—some more than others, and some more intensely than others—a longing this world cannot satisfy, a sense that there must be more.

The Rationalist

We turn now to Lewis's rationalism. And, as with the term *romanticism*, I mean something different from some of its common philosophical uses. All I mean is his profound devotion to being rational—to the principle that there is true rationality and that it is rooted in absolute Reason.

Remember that the subtitle of *The Pilgrim's Regress* is *An Allegorical Apology for Christianity, Reason, and Romanticism*. We've seen what he meant by *romanticism*. Now what was his defense of reason?

Logic Leading beyond Nature

The simplest way to get at the heart of Lewis's rationality is to say he believed in the law of noncontradiction, and he believed that where this law was abandoned, not only was truth imperiled but romanticism and Joy were imperiled as well. The law of noncontradiction is simply that contradictory statements cannot both be true at the same time and in the same way.

---

[23] C. S. Lewis, *The Problem of Pain* (New York: Macmillan, 1962), 145–46.

Lewis saw logic as a real expression of ultimate reality. The laws of logic are not human conventions created differently from culture to culture. They are rooted in the way God is. And these laws of logic make true knowledge of reality possible. "I conclude then," he writes, "that logic is a real insight into the way in which real things have to exist. In other words, the laws of thought are also the laws of things: of things in the remotest space and the remotest time."[24]

Two Paths to One Place

This commitment to the basic laws of logic, or rationality, led Lewis on the philosophical path to the same Christ that he had found on the path of romanticism or Joy. He put it like this: "This lived dialectic [of my romanticism], and the merely argued dialectic of my philosophical progress, seem to have converged on one goal,"[25] namely, the reality of theism, and Christianity, and Christ as the Savior of the world.

On the romantic path, Lewis was led again and again to look beyond nature for ultimate reality—finally to God in Christ—because his desires could not be explained as a product of this world. Now how did that same thing happen by the use of his reason?

He looked at the philosophical, scientific cosmology emerging in the modern world and found it self-contradictory.

> If I swallow the scientific cosmology as a whole (that excludes a rational, personal God), then not only can I not fit in Christianity, but I cannot even fit in science. If minds are wholly dependent on brains, and brains on biochemistry, and biochemistry (in the long run) on the meaningless flux of the atoms, I cannot understand how the thought of those minds should have any more significance than the sound of the wind in the trees. And this is to me the final test.[26]

In other words, modern people construct a worldview that treats their thoughts as equivalent to wind in the trees. And then they call

---

[24] C. S. Lewis, "*De Futilitate*" in *Essay Collection and Other Short Pieces* (London: HarperCollins, 2000), 674.
[25] Lewis, *The Pilgrim's Regress*, 10.
[26] C. S. Lewis, "Is Theology Poetry?," in *Essay Collection and Other Short Pieces*, 21.

these thoughts true. Lewis said that's a contradiction. Atheistic man uses his mind to create a worldview that nullifies the use of his mind.

The Abolition of Man

This is what Lewis meant by the title of his book *The Abolition of Man*. If there is no God as the foundation of logic (as with the law of noncontradiction) and the foundation of value judgments (such as for justice and beauty), then man is abolished. His mind is no more than the rustling of leaves, and his value judgments are no more than ripples on a pond.

> The rebellion of new ideologies against the Tao [the absoluteness of first principles—and ultimately against God] is a rebellion of the branches against the tree: if the rebels could succeed they would find that they had destroyed themselves.[27]

Lewis compares atheistic cosmology to dreaming and Christian theology to being awake. When you are awake, you can explain wakefulness and dreaming. But when you are dreaming, you don't have the capacity to explain wakefulness. Similarly,

> Christian theology can fit in science, art, morality, and the sub-Christian religions. The scientific point of view cannot fit in any of these things, not even science itself. I believe in Christianity as I believe that the Sun has risen: not only because I see it but because by it I see everything else.[28]

From Reason to Christianity

Here's how he described the way these thoughts brought him on the path of reason to see Christianity as true:

> On these grounds and others like them one is driven to think that whatever else may be true, the popular scientific cosmology at any rate is certainly not. . . . Something like philosophical idealism or Theism must, at the very worst, be less untrue than that. And

---

[27] C. S. Lewis, *The Abolition of Man* (New York: Macmillan, 1947), 56.
[28] Lewis, "Is Theology Poetry?," 21.

idealism turned out, when you took it seriously, to be disguised Theism. And once you accepted Theism you could not ignore the claims of Christ. And when you examine them it appeared to be that you could adopt no middle position. Either he was a lunatic or God. And he was not a lunatic.[29]

So we have seen that both Lewis's romanticism and his rationalism brought him to Christ. His lifelong, recurrent experience of the in-breaking of a longing he could not explain by this world led beyond the world to God and finally to Christ. And his lifelong experience of reason and logic led him to see that truth and beauty and justice and science would have no validity at all if there were no transcendent God in whom they were all rooted.

A Master Likener

Therefore, Lewis came to Christ as his Lord and God along the path of *romanticism*, or inconsolable longing, on the one hand, and the path of *rationalism*, or logic, on the other hand. Both of these experiences demanded of him that he own the reality of something beyond this material world, something Other, something More than this world. Both paths finally converged on Jesus Christ as the creator, redeemer, and supreme fulfillment of all our longings, and the ground of all our reasoning.

Both romanticism and rationalism—longing and logic—led him out of this world to find the meaning and validity of this world. This world could not satisfy his deepest desires. And this world could not give validity to his plainest logic. Desires found full and lasting satisfaction, and the truth-claims of reason found legitimacy in God, not in this world.

A Key to the Power of Language

This double experience of romanticism and rationalism, leading finally to God, gave to Lewis a key to the power of language to reveal

---

[29] Ibid., 20.

the deeper meaning of the world, namely, the key of *likening*. What I mean by the key of likening is this: *Likening some aspect of reality to what it is not can reveal more of what it is.*

God created what is not God. He made not-God the means of revealing and knowing God. And Lewis found the key to what the world really is by being led out of the world to something other than the world, namely, God. He found that this world is most honest and most true when it is pointing beyond itself.

He reasoned like this: if the key to the deepest meaning of this world lies outside this world, then the world will probably be illumined most deeply not simply by describing the world as what it is, but by likening the world to what it is not.

Unremitting Rational Clarity

Part of what makes Lewis so illuminating on almost everything he touches is his unremitting *rational clarity* and his pervasive use of *likening*. Metaphor, analogy, illustration, simile, poetry, story, myth—all of these are ways of *likening* aspects of reality to what it is *not* for the sake of showing more deeply what it *is*.

At one level, it seems paradoxical to liken something to what it is *not* in order to show more deeply what it *is*. But that's what life had taught Lewis. And he devoted his whole life to exemplifying and defending this truth. He wrote to T. S. Eliot in 1931 to explain an essay he had sent him and said, "The whole [of it], when completed . . . will re-affirm the romantic doctrine of *imagination as a truth-bearing faculty*, though not quite as the romantics understood it."[30]

The Paradoxical Effect of Likening

Lewis had experienced this all his life—the power of verbal images to illumine reality. But when he became a Christian, this deep-seated way of seeing the world was harnessed for the sake of

---

[30] C. S. Lewis, *The Collected Letters of C. S. Lewis, vol. 3: Narnia, Cambridge, and Joy, 1950–1963*, ed. Walter Hooper (San Francisco: HarperSanFrancisco, 2007), 1,523 (emphasis added).

illumining truth in everything he wrote. In 1954 Lewis sent a list of his books to the Milton Society of America and explained what ties them together:

> The imaginative man in me is older, more continuously operative, and in that sense more basic than either the religious writer or the critic. It was he who made me first attempt (with little success) to be a poet. . . . It was he who after my conversion led me to embody my religious belief in symbolical or mythopeic [*sic*] forms, rang- ing from *Screwtape* to a kind of theologised science-fiction. And it was of course he who has brought me, in the last few years, to write the series of Narnian stories for children.[31]

He tells us in more than one place why he embraced imaginative literature as such a large part of his calling. All these forms of liken- ing have the paradoxical effect of revealing aspects of the real that we often otherwise miss.

Imagination and Reality

In 1940 he wrote in a letter, "Mythologies . . . are products of imagina- tion in the sense that their content is *imaginative*. The more *imagina- tive* ones are 'near the mark' in the sense that *they communicate more Reality to us*."[32] In other words, by likening reality to what it is not, we learn more of what it is.

In his essay "On Stories," Lewis comments on the ancient myth of *Oedipus* and says, "It may not be 'like real life' in the superficial sense: but it sets before us an image of what reality may well be like at some more central region."[33]

Lewis calls Tolkien's Lord of the Rings a "great romance,"[34] and comments in a letter in 1958, "A great romance is like a flower whose smell reminds you of something you can't quite place. . . .

---

[31] Ibid., 516–17.
[32] C. S. Lewis, *The Collected Letters of C. S. Lewis, vol. 2: Books, Broadcasts and War, 1931–1949*, ed. Walter Hooper (San Francisco: HarperCollins, 2007), 445 (emphasis added).
[33] C. S. Lewis, "On Stories," in *Essay Collection and Other Short Pieces*, 501.
[34] Lewis, *Collected Letters, vol. 3*, 371.

I've never met Orcs or Ents or Elves—but the feel of it, the sense of a huge past, of lowering danger, of heroic tasks achieved by the most apparently unheroic people, of distance, vastness, strangeness, homeliness (all blended together) is so exactly what living feels like to me."[35]

Revealing Reality

In the preface to *The Pilgrim's Regress*, he comments, "All good allegory exists not to hide but to reveal; to make the inner world more palpable by giving it an (imagined) concrete embodiment."[36] And in his poem "Impenitence," he defends imaginary talking animals by saying they are,

> Masks for Man, cartoons, parodies by Nature
>   Formed to reveal us.

In other words, heroic myth and penetrating allegory and great romance and talking animals are "masks . . . formed to reveal." Again the paradox of likening—depicting *some aspect of reality as what it is not in order to reveal more of what it is.*

Likening in Apologetics

But lest I give the wrong impression that Lewis was a likener only in his poetry and fiction, I need to stress that he was a likener everywhere—in everything he wrote. Myths and allegories and romances and fairy tales are extended metaphors. But thinking and writing metaphorically and imaginatively and analogically were present everywhere in Lewis's life and work.

Lewis was a poet and craftsman and image maker in everything he wrote. Alister McGrath observed that what captivated the reader of Lewis's sermons and essays and apologetic works, not just his novels, was

---

[35] Ibid., 971–72.
[36] Lewis, *Pilgrim's Regress*, 13.

his ability to write prose tinged with a poetic vision, its carefully crafted phrases lingering in the memory because they have captivated the imagination. The qualities we associate with good poetry—such as an appreciation of the sound of words, rich and suggestive analogies and images, vivid description, and lyrical sense—are found in Lewis's prose.[37]

I think this is exactly right, and it makes him not only refreshing and illuminating to read on almost any topic but also a great model for how to think and write about everything.

Walter Hooper puts it like this:

A sampling of all Lewis's works will reveal the same man in his poetry as in his clear and sparkling prose. His wonderful imagination is the guiding thread. It is continuously at work. . . . And this is why, I think, his admirers find it so pleasant to be instructed by him in subjects they have hitherto cared so little for. Everything he touched had his kind of magic about it.[38]

It is indeed pleasant to be instructed by a master likener. Images and analogies and creative illustrations and metaphors and surprising turns of phrase are pleasant. "A word fitly spoken is like apples of gold in a setting of silver" (Prov. 25:11). Solomon even uses an image to celebrate the pleasure of images. But my point here has not been the *pleasure* of likening, but its power of *illumination*. Its power to reveal truth.

The Key to Deepest Meaning

Lewis's romanticism and his rationalism—his inconsolable longing and his validity-demanding logic—pointed outside the world for the key to understanding the world. And he found that if the key to the deepest meaning of this world lies outside this world—in its maker and redeemer, Jesus Christ—then the world itself will probably be

---

[37] McGrath, *C. S. Lewis*, 108.
[38] Walter Hooper, *Poems* (Orlando, FL: Harcourt, 1992), *vi*.

illumined most deeply not simply by describing the world merely as what it is but by *likening* the world to what it's not.

Lewis's unrelenting commitment to *likening*—to the use of images and analogies and metaphor and surprising juxtapositions, even in his most logical demonstrations of truth—was not mainly owing to the greater pleasure it can give but to the deeper truth it can reveal. Lewis loved the truth. He loved objective reality. He believed that the truth of this world and the truth of God can be known. He believed that the use of reason is essential in knowing and defending truth. But he also believed that there are depths of truth and dimensions of reality that *likening* will reveal more deeply than reason.

Seeing Wonder in This World

Unless we see that this world is not ultimate reality but is only like it, we will not see and savor this world for the wonder that it is. Lewis is at his metaphorical best as he explains this with his image-laden prose in this paragraph from *Miracles*:

> The Englishness of English is audible only to those who know some other language as well. In the same way and for the same reason, only Supernaturalists really see Nature. You must go a little way from her, and then turn round, and look back. Then at last the true landscape will become visible. You must have tasted, however briefly, the pure water from beyond the world before you can be distinctly conscious of the hot, salty tang of Nature's current. To treat her as God, or as Everything, is to lose the whole pith and pleasure of her [note: pith *and* pleasure]. Come out, look back, and then you will see . . . this astonishing cataract of bears, babies, and bananas: this immoderate deluge of atoms, orchids, oranges, cancers, canaries, fleas, gases, tornadoes, and toads. How could you have ever thought this was ultimate reality? How could you ever have thought that it was merely a stage-set for the moral drama of men and women? She is herself. Offer her neither worship nor contempt. Meet her and know her. . . . The theologians

tell us that she, like ourselves, is to be redeemed. The "vanity" to which she was subjected was her disease, not her essence. She will be cured, but cured in character: not tamed (Heaven forbid) nor sterilized. We shall still be able to recognize our old enemy, friend, play-fellow and foster-mother, so perfected as to be not less, but more, herself. And that will be a merry meeting.[39]

"Only Supernaturalists really see nature." The only people who can know the terrifying wonder of the world are those who know that the world is not the most wonderful and terrifying reality. The world is a likening. The path of romanticism taught Lewis that the world is a likening—the final satisfaction of our longing is not in this world. The path of rationality taught Lewis that the world is a likening. The final validation of our thinking is not in this world. And since this world is a likening—not the goal of our longing or the ground of our logic—therefore it is revealed for what it most profoundly is by likening.

The Evangelist

What was Lewis doing in all his works—in all his likening and in all his likening-soaked reasoning? He was pointing. He was unveiling. He was depicting the glory of God in the face of Jesus. He was leading people to Christ. The two paths he knew best were the paths of romanticism and rationalism—longing and logic. So these are the paths on which he guided people to Christ.

One of the things that makes him admirable to me, in spite of all our doctrinal differences, is his crystal clear, unashamed belief that people are lost without Christ and that every Christian should try to win them, including world-class scholars of medieval and Renaissance literature. And so, unlike many tentative, hidden, vague, approval-craving intellectual Christians, Lewis says outright, "The salvation of a single soul is more important than the production or

---

[39] C. S. Lewis, *Miracles: A Preliminary Study* (New York: Macmillan, 1947), 67–68.

preservation of all the epics and tragedies in the world."[40] And again: "The glory of God, and, as our only means to glorifying Him, the salvation of human souls, is the real business of life."[41]

Helping Us See Glory

This is what he was doing in all his likening and all his reasoning. And when Norman Pittenger criticized him in 1958 for being simplistic in his portrayal of Christian faith, Lewis responded in a way that shows us what he was doing in all his work:

> When I began, Christianity came before the great mass of my unbelieving fellow-countrymen either in the highly emotional form offered by revivalists or in the unintelligible language of highly cultured clergymen. Most men were reached by neither. My task was therefore simply that of a translator—one turning Christian doctrine, or what he believed to be such, into the vernacular, into language that unscholarly people would attend to and could understand. . . . Dr Pittenger would be a more helpful critic if he advised a cure as well as asserting many diseases. How does he himself do such work? What methods, and with what success, does he employ when he is trying to convert the great mass of storekeepers, lawyers, realtors, morticians, policemen and artisans who surround him in his own city?[42]

Lewis came to Christ on the converging paths of romanticism and rationalism. And as a Christian, he became a master thinker and master likener. This is who he was, and this is what he knew. And so this is how he did his evangelism. He bent every romantic effort and every rational effort to help people see what he had seen—the glory of Jesus Christ, the goal of all his longings, and the solid ground of all his thoughts.

---

[40] C. S. Lewis, "Christianity and Literature," in *Christian Reflections* (Grand Rapids, MI: Eerdmans, 1967), 10.
[41] C. S. Lewis, "Christianity and Culture," in *Christian Reflections*, 14.
[42] C. S. Lewis, "Rejoinder to Dr Pittenger," in *God in the Dock* (Grand Rapids, MI: Eerdmans, 1970), 183.

2

INERRANCY AND THE PATRON SAINT OF EVANGELICALISM

C. S. Lewis on Holy Scripture

PHILIP RYKEN

At the beginning of *The Silver Chair*, young Jill Pole finds herself in a wood at the top of a high mountain. There she meets a lion, who gives her the task of finding a lost prince and bringing him back home to Narnia.

The lion also gives Jill four signs to guide her on this quest. When he asks her to repeat these four signs, she does not remember them quite as well as she expected. So the lion corrects her and then patiently asks her to repeat the signs until she can say them word-perfect, and in the proper order.

Unfortunately, even though she knows the signs by heart, Jill somehow manages to forget most of them by the time she needs them. The first sign pertains to Jill's traveling companion—a boy named Eustace Clarence Scrubb (and who almost deserved it). As soon as Eustace sets foot in Narnia, he will meet a dear old friend, whom he is to greet at once so he can gain help for his journey. But by the time the children figure out that the old king of Narnia actually is Eustace's friend Caspian, the king has sailed away, and they have missed their chance. "We've muffed the first sign," Jill says impatiently. "And now . . . everything is going wrong from the very beginning."[1] And so it continues. Later in the story, when the children discover to their dismay that they have also muffed the second and third signs, Jill admits, "It's my fault. I—I'd given up repeating [them] every night."[2]

Whether C. S. Lewis meant it this way or not, to me this story has always illustrated the importance and challenge of Holy Scripture in the Christian life—of memorizing Bible verses, spending time in God's Word every day, and putting what it says into practice. To be faithful to her calling, Jill needed to go back every day to the will of Aslan (for, of course, he was the lion who sent her on the quest). Yet, as time went on, she was tempted to neglect the daily practice of reciting the four signs. And because of this neglect, she and her friends fell into disobedience and confusion, nearly to the point of death.

If there *is* an analogy here, then it is entirely in keeping with the importance that C. S. Lewis placed on biblical truth for Christian discipleship. For Lewis, Holy Scripture was the supreme authority for faith and practice, and reading the Bible had life-giving influence for the Christian. These writings are "holy," Lewis said, "inspired," "the Oracles of God."[3] The way for us to know God is on the authority of his Word, which provides the data for doing theology.[4]

A Few Shortcomings

These strong affirmations of Scripture may seem surprising. Although some evangelicals quote C. S. Lewis on almost everything else, usually we do not quote him on the inspiration and authority of the Bible. This is because Lewis's doctrine of Scripture has long been regarded as something less than fully orthodox.

Presumably that is one of the main reasons for including this

---

[1] C. S. Lewis, *The Silver Chair* (London: Collins, 1974), 47.
[2] Ibid., 109.
[3] C. S. Lewis, *Reflections on the Psalms* (London: Geoffrey Bles, 1958), 109.
[4] C. S. Lewis, "Letters to Malcolm," Bodleian Library, University of Oxford, Dep. D. 808, 48.

chapter in a book-length appreciation of C. S. Lewis. Is it possible to make sense of the puzzling inconsistencies in Lewis's writing on the nature and origin of sacred Scripture? One is reminded of the question that *Christianity Today* once posed about C. S. Lewis, as to how "a man whose theology had decidedly un-evangelical elements has come to be the Aquinas, the Augustine, and the Aesop of contemporary evangelicalism."[5]

When it comes to "un-evangelical elements" in Lewis's theology, his views on the Bible are near the top of the list. My purpose here is to be honest about several shortcomings in his doctrine of Scripture and then to qualify those shortcomings by setting them in the context of Lewis's thought as a whole, before finally mentioning some of the strengths of his approach to the Bible that can help nourish our own confidence in the Word of God.

He Downplayed the Bible's Uniqueness

So here is a first shortcoming: *C. S. Lewis placed the inspiration of Scripture on a continuum with other forms of literary inspiration, thus downplaying to some degree the uniqueness of the Bible.*

As a professor of English, Lewis rightly saw many similarities between the books of the Bible and other forms of literature. Indeed, as we shall see, his sensitivity to the Bible's literary qualities is one of his greatest strengths as a lay theologian. But his appreciation for these similarities also caused him to underestimate the unique origin of Holy Scripture in the mind of the Holy Spirit.

In an important letter to Clyde Kilby, who then chaired the English department at Wheaton College, Lewis reasoned, "If every good and perfect gift comes from the Father of Lights then all true and edifying writings, whether in Scripture or not, must be *in some sense* inspired."[6] The question, of course, is in *what* sense are they inspired.

---

[5] "Still Surprised by Lewis," *Christianity Today* (September 1998), 54.
[6] C. S. Lewis, letter to Clyde S. Kilby, May 7, 1959, in *The Collected Letters of C. S. Lewis, vol. 3: Narnia, Cambridge, and Joy, 1950–1963*, ed. Walter Hooper (San Francisco: HarperSanFrancisco, 2007), 1,045 (emphasis original).

Elsewhere, Lewis used Homer as an example of a poet who was in-spired by invoking his muse and quoted Ralph Waldo Emerson's declaration "that there was a good deal of inspiration in a chest of good tea."[7] Is this all that we mean when we say that Moses, Paul, and the other biblical writers were "inspired"?

Lewis recognized that the word *inspiration* is not self-defining. This term "has been misunderstood in more than one way," he wrote, "and I must try to explain how I understand it."[8] Part of his explana-tion was that even within the canon of Scripture, there are various degrees and different modes of inspiration. Not only is Scripture on a continuum with other works of literature, therefore, but within the Bible itself, some books are more fully inspired than others. Lewis tended to think of inspiration "as a Divine pressure that God exerted on all the biblical authors, but not in the same way or to the same degree."[9] Obviously, the words of Jesus are the most inspired, fol-lowed perhaps by the writings of the apostle Paul, which come more directly from God than the writings of the Old Testament.[10] So, for Lewis, the rationalist, "all Holy Scripture is in some sense—though not all parts of it in the same sense—the word of God."[11]

Michael Christensen, who regards Lewis as holding a mediating view between liberalism and evangelicalism, uses the phrase "liter-ary inspiration" to describe Lewis's doctrine of Scripture.[12] But how-ever we describe it, Lewis held to something less than the *plenary verbal inspiration* that has been normative for evangelical theology. *Plenary* means "full"—the whole Bible is inspired. *Verbal* refers to the very words of the Bible—every word in Holy Scripture is equally inspired by God.

---

[7] C. S. Lewis and E. M. W. Tillyard, *The Personal Heresy: A Controversy* (London: Oxford University Press, 1939), 23.

[8] Lewis, *Reflections on the Psalms*, 109.

[9] Christopher W. Mitchell, "Lewis and Historic Evangelicalism," in *C. S. Lewis and the Church: Essays in Honour of Walter Hooper*, ed. Judith Wolfe and Brendan N. Wolfe (London: Bloomsbury, 2012), 165. The term "Divine pressure" appears in *Reflections on the Psalms*, 111.

[10] Lewis, *Reflections on the Psalms*, 112–13.

[11] Ibid., 19.

[12] Michael J. Christensen, *C. S. Lewis on Scripture: His Thoughts on the Nature of Biblical Inspiration, the Role of Revelation, and the Question of Inerrancy* (Nashville, TN: Abingdon, 1979), 77.

The classic expression of plenary verbal inspiration appears in 2 Timothy 3:16: "All Scripture is breathed out by God." This verse does not say merely that God inspired the men who wrote the Bible; it says rather that God inspired the Bible itself, with the result that its words are his words. Because "all" Scripture is breathed out by God, such divine inspiration extends to every word. Thus there can be no degrees of inspiration within the canon. The Bible's words are God's words.

At times, Lewis takes instead what seems to be an adoptionist view of Scripture, in which merely human writings are incorporated into the Bible and used for divine purposes. God consecrates the secular to make it sacred. In one of his letters, Lewis drew an analogy to the humanity and the deity of Jesus Christ. "I myself think of [inspiration] as analogous to the Incarnation," he wrote, "as in Christ a human soul-and-body are taken up and made the vehicle of Deity, so in Scripture, a mass of human legend, history, moral teaching etc. are taken up and made the vehicle of God's Word."[13] Although it is not divine, but human in its origin, biblical literature has been "raised by God above itself, qualified by Him to serve purposes which of itself it would not have served."[14] Similarly, in his *Reflections on the Psalms*, Lewis claims that the Bible is not "the conversion of God's word into a literature," but the "taking up of a literature to be a vehicle of God's word."[15] This claim makes the inspiration a divine response rather than what it actually is: a divine initiative, in which God speaks through human words.

He Believed There Were Contradictions and Errors

A second shortcoming in Lewis's doctrine of Scripture is that he *believed there were contradictions and probably errors in the Bible*. Here we go beyond inspiration to address a second key component in the evangelical doctrine of Scripture, namely, inerrancy. Inspiration is a claim about the Bible's source: it comes from the Holy Spirit. Inerrancy is a claim about the Bible's content: it is free from error.

---

[13] C. S. Lewis, letter to Lee Turner, July 19, 1958, *Collected Letters, vol. 3*, 961.
[14] Lewis, *Reflections on the Psalms*, 111.
[15] Ibid., 116.

Lewis hints at his discomfort with biblical inerrancy in the Kilby letter mentioned previously. Kilby had sent Lewis a copy of the "Wheaton College Statement Concerning the Inspiration of the Bible" and asked for his opinion. In reply, Lewis listed a series of facts that would have to be accounted for in any doctrine of biblical authority. The list included what Lewis described as "the apparent inconsistencies" between the genealogies in Matthew 1 and Luke 3 and between the accounts of the death of Judas Iscariot in Matthew 27:5 and Acts 1:18–19.[16]

Although Lewis was careful not to use the word *error* in the Kilby correspondence, he did use it in one of his earlier letters. "Errors of minor fact are permitted to remain" in Scripture, he wrote. "One must remember of course that our modern and western attention to dates, numbers, etc. simply did not exist in the ancient world. No one was looking for *that* sort of truth."[17] Thus, the Bible is not the word of God "in the sense that every passage, in itself, gives impeccable science of history."[18] To give a more specific example, the large numbers given for the armies of Israel in the Old Testament led Lewis to rule out "the view that any one passage taken in isolation can be assumed to be inerrant in exactly the same sense as any other." "The very *kind* of truth we are often demanding was," in his opinion, "never even envisaged by the ancients."[19]

Minor factual errors were not troubling to Lewis; nor did they diminish his confidence in the overall truthfulness of the Bible. In his book *The Problem of Pain* he claimed, "If our Lord had committed himself to any scientific or historical statement which we knew to be untrue, this would not disturb my faith in His deity."[20] In saying this, Lewis did not actually attribute any error to the words of Jesus, but he was saying that discovering certain errors would not threaten the core of Christian orthodoxy. He went further in his essay "The

---

[16] Lewis, letter to Kilby, *Collected Letters, vol. 3*, 1,045.
[17] Lewis, letter to Turner, *Collected Letters, vol. 3*, 961 (emphasis original).
[18] Lewis, *Reflections on the Psalms*, 112.
[19] Lewis, letter to Kilby, *Collected Letters, vol. 3*, 1,046 (emphasis original).
[20] C. S. Lewis, *The Problem of Pain* (New York: Macmillan, 1944), 117.

World's Last Night." There, in addressing the seeming discrepancy between the disciples' expectation of the imminent return of Jesus Christ and the actual timing of the second coming, Lewis said that Jesus "shared, and indeed created, their delusion."[21]

He Doubted or Denied Certain Parts as Historical

A third shortcoming is closely related to the second: *C. S. Lewis doubted or denied that certain parts of the Bible were historical, including books that evangelicals traditionally have regarded as historical narrative.*

In the list that Lewis sent to Kilby—the list of factors to be accounted for in any doctrine of Scripture—item four read as follows: "The universally admitted unhistoricity (I do not say, of course, falsity) of at least some narratives in scripture (the parables), which may well extend also to Jonah and Job." Lewis made similar comments elsewhere. To begin at the beginning, he was open to the possibility that the creation account in Genesis was derived from pagan literature.[22] Do the opening chapters of the Bible give us reliable history? What about the fall, for example? Lewis was far from certain. "For all I can see," he wrote, "it might have concerned the literal eating of a fruit, but the question is of no consequence."[23] He said something similar about the book of Ruth and the question of its historicity. "I've no reason to suppose it is *not*,"[24] he says, which is hardly a ringing endorsement. In writing to Corbin Scott Carnell, and commenting specifically on Jonah and Esther, Lewis confessed that he was uneasy about "attributing the same kind and degree of historicity to all the books of the Bible."[25] Or consider this, again on the book of Jonah: "The author quite obviously writes as a storyteller not as a chronicler."[26]

As we shall see, Lewis issued a staunch defense of many biblical

---

[21] C. S. Lewis, *The World's Last Night and Other Essays* (New York: Harcourt, Brace, 1960), 98.
[22] Lewis, *Reflections on the Psalms*, 110.
[23] Lewis, *The Problem of Pain*, 68.
[24] Lewis, letter to Kilby, *Collected Letters, vol. 3*, 1,044 (emphasis original).
[25] C. S. Lewis, letter to Corbin Scott Carnell, April 5, 1953, *Collected Letters, vol. 3*, 319.
[26] Lewis, *Reflections on the Psalms*, 110.

narratives—especially the resurrection of Jesus Christ and other miracles. But when it came to certain Bible stories—and here he offered "the fate of Lot's wife" as an example—the value of their historicity mattered to him "hardly at all." So how can we tell the difference between the stories in which history matters and the stories in which it doesn't? The stories "whose historicity matters," Lewis wrote, "are those where it is plain."[27] Unfortunately, this is not a criterion that can stand up to much scrutiny. Plainness, like beauty, is in the eye of the beholder!

Nearly everything we have seen so far in Lewis's views on the inspiration, inerrancy, and historicity of Scripture is summarized in a famous quotation from his *Reflections on the Psalms*, in which he claimed that within Israel's hymnal, "the human qualities of the raw materials show through. Naivety, error, contradiction, even (as in the cursing Psalms) wickedness are not removed. The total result is not 'the Word of God' in the sense that every passage, in itself, gives impeccable science or history. It carries the Word of God," conveying this Word to the reader, who "also needs His inspiration."[28] Here Lewis comes perilously close to a neoorthodox view of Scripture, in which the biblical text is not inherently divine but only becomes the Word of God when the Spirit of God makes it so for the reader.

Given these shortcomings on Scripture, it is not surprising that Lewis declined to endorse conventional evangelical terminology for the doctrine of Scripture. Nor should it be surprising that evangelicals generally did not regard him as a reliable ally in "the battle for the Bible" that raged during the 1970s and 80s.

Garry Friesen has aptly described Lewis's doctrine of Scripture as "suborthodox."[29] Even if he did not develop a systematic theology of Scripture that could fairly be described as "liberal," or even "neoorthodox," some of the statements Lewis made about the inspiration and accuracy of Scripture fell short of biblical orthodoxy—not just

---

[27] Lewis, letter to Kilby, *Collected Letters*, vol. 3, 1,045.

[28] Lewis, *Reflections on the Psalms*, 94.

[29] Garry L. Friesen, "Scripture in the Writings of C. S. Lewis," *Evangelical Journal*, vol. 1 (1983): 24.

evangelical orthodoxy but also the orthodoxy of mere Christianity. Since the time of Christ, genuine believers in every theological tradition have received the Bible as the true and perfect Word of God.

What makes Lewis's "suborthodoxy" especially concerning, of course, is his extraordinary influence. For many readers, C. S. Lewis has been the first introduction to Christianity, or else the first reliable guide in living the Christian life. Evangelicals rightly have been concerned that his popularity might promote a less than orthodox doctrine of Scripture.

Some Qualifications

Yet before rejecting everything that C. S. Lewis ever said about Holy Scripture, we should put his views in context and, with Christian charity, give them some of the qualifications they deserve.

Not a "Real Theologian"

It is important to remember that Lewis was not a theologian but a literary critic. Thus he often reminded his readers of the limits of his knowledge of historical theology and deferred to scholars in other fields (especially the "real theologians," as he called them).[30] For example, in *Fern-seed and Elephants*, he located himself with a group of "outsiders" to biblical studies—Bible readers who were "educated, but not theologically educated."[31] And in *The World's Last Night*, as he offered his surprising perspective on the second coming of Jesus Christ, he gave the following caution: "I have no claim to speak as an expert and merely put forward the reflections which have arisen in my own mind and have seemed to me (perhaps wrongly) to be helpful. They are all submitted to the correction of wiser heads."[32]

Lewis gave similar caveats when he was commenting on the doctrine of Scripture. As he admitted to one of his correspondents,

---

[30] C. S. Lewis, *Transposition and Other Addresses* (London: Geoffrey Bles, 1949), 19.
[31] C. S. Lewis, "Modern Theology and Biblical Criticism," in *Christian Reflections*, ed. Walter Hooper (Grand Rapids, MI: Eerdmans, 1967), 152–53.
[32] Lewis, *World's Last Night*, 93–94.

"I cannot claim to have a clearly worked out position about the Bible or the nature of Inspiration. That is a subject on which I would gladly learn: I have nothing to teach."[33]

We should take these comments seriously. Given Lewis's awareness of his own limits, it is perhaps unfair to subject his views to the kind of rigorous critique we would give a systematic theologian. Lewis himself would discourage us from basing our own doctrine of Scripture on his views, which are not always consistent anyway. As Kevin Vanhoozer wisely observes, "It is difficult to extract a 'doctrine' of scripture from Lewis's occasional writings, for Lewis was less interested in critical approaches to, or doctrines of, scripture than he was in the realities about which scripture speaks."[34]

We should also recognize the significance of the fact that Lewis's most serious reservations about the Bible do not appear in his published writings but in personal letters. Because he knew that he did not have all the answers, he was careful about what he said or wrote in public, where it seems that he never addressed the question of inerrancy as a category of systematic theology.

One omission is particularly telling. The original manuscript for *Letters to Malcolm: Chiefly on Prayer* includes one entire chapter that was never published. The subject of the chapter was biblical inerrancy, and in it Lewis gives some of his reasons for "disbelieving" in the literal inspiration of Holy Scripture. He argues that parts of the Bible—the Gospel of Luke, for example—come from human inquiry rather than through spiritual revelation. He also claims that the Bible contains contradictions of historical fact. Perhaps more importantly, some parts of the Bible—Job is the clearest example, as he is a man who "lives in a country we know nothing about, at a wholly undetermined period"[35]—do not claim to be factual at all. These argu-

---

[33] C. S. Lewis, letter to Edward T. Dell, February 4, 1949, *The Collected Letters of C. S. Lewis, vol. 2: Books, Broadcasts, and the War, 1931–1949*, ed. Walter Hooper (San Francisco: HarperCollins, 2004), 914.
[34] Kevin J. Vanhoozer, "On scripture," in *The Cambridge Companion to C. S. Lewis*, ed. Robert MacSwain and Michael Ward (Cambridge, UK: Cambridge University Press, 2011), 75.
[35] The manuscript "Letters to Malcolm" is held in the collections of the Bodleian Library at the University of Oxford, Dep. D. 808, pp. 48–50. A facsimile is available for researchers at the Marion E. Wade Center at Wheaton College, Wheaton, Illinois.

ments are hardly new, as they are familiar to anyone who knows Lewis's correspondence. The manuscript is important rather for what it reveals about Lewis's reticence to publish his thoughts on biblical inerrancy.

Lewis had exercised similar caution in his letter to Kilby, where he was careful not to claim that he had developed a thoroughly reliable doctrine of Scripture. In fact, he described his views on inerrancy as "pretty tentative, much less an attempt to establish a view than statement of the issue on which, rightly or wrongly, I have come to work." He also requested that if Kilby thought his letter "at all likely to upset anyone," he would kindly "throw it in the waste paper basket."[36]

In the end, of course, C. S. Lewis bears responsibility for what he did write about Scripture. Every author has that responsibility, which is why the apostle James warned that not many of us should become teachers (James 3:1). But we also need to take Lewis's qualifications seriously. When he tells us that he is not a theologian or that he is giving only his tentative thoughts, he means what he says. We should both admire and emulate his teachable spirit.

It is hard not to wonder how much C. S. Lewis might have been helped by doing more extensive study on the doctrine of Scripture. His shortcomings on Scripture come in no small measure from failing to read the right books—a fault he sometimes pointed out in others. One early critic described his "refusal to acquaint himself with responsible Biblical criticism" as "almost inexcusable."[37] But we should bear in mind that Lewis spent the majority of his time reading dramas, epic poems, and other great works of literature (as an English professor should). He owned barely a handful of books on the doctrine of Scripture. He read G. B. Bentley's *The Resurrection of the Bible*, for example, and C. H. Dodd's less conservative book *The Authority of the Bible*. But, as far as we know, he never read anything like B. B. Warfield's seminal writings on the inspiration and authority of Scripture.

---

[36] Lewis, letter to Kilby, *Collected Letters*, vol. 3, 1,044.
[37] Richard B. Cunningham, *C. S. Lewis: Defender of the Faith* (Philadelphia: Westminster, 1967), 94.

Nor did Lewis live long enough to encounter the Chicago Statement on Biblical Inerrancy—a document that offers a robust defense
of biblical authority while at the same time making some of the very
nuances that were important to Lewis. The Chicago Statement and
the related documents produced by the International Council of Biblical Inerrancy (ICBI) recognize that the Bible contains a variety of
literary genres. No evangelical expects a parable to be historical, for
example. Nor does the doctrine of inerrancy claim that everything
in the Bible is a fact but only that when the Bible does present a
fact, that fact is true. This is perfectly in keeping with Lewis's own
insistence that every work of literature should be read as the kind
of literature it is. Not everything in the Bible claims to be historical;
only the history does. The ICBI documents also recognize that some
ancient cultures used large numbers rather unscientifically—another
concern of Lewis's. So at least some of his reservations about biblical
inerrancy were later addressed by qualifications held by a majority
of evangelical scholars today.

The doctrine of Scripture that Lewis disagreed with was not so
much evangelical as it was fundamentalist—or at least what some
people believe is fundamentalist. In one letter he clarified, "My own
position is not Fundamentalist, if Fundamentalism means accepting
as a point of faith at the outset the proposition 'Every statement in
the Bible is completely true in the literal, historical sense.' That would
break down at once on the parables." So far, so good. Any evangelical would agree, and most fundamentalists would as well. But then
Lewis went on to say this:

> All the same commonsense and general understanding of literary
> kinds which would forbid anyone to take the parables as his-
> torical statements, carried a very little further, would force us to
> distinguish between (1.) Books like *Acts* or the account of Da-
> vid's reign, which are everywhere dovetailed into a known his-
> tory, geography, and genealogies (2.) Books like *Esther*, or *Jonah*
> or *Job* which deal with otherwise unknown characters living in

unspecified periods, and pretty well *proclaim* themselves to be sacred fiction.[38]

Here Lewis uses his judgments about literary genre to press the traditional understanding of certain biblical books. He is not saying that the history we read in the Bible is inaccurate. But he is saying that some books of the Bible, which evangelicals traditionally have regarded as history, are not meant to be history at all. They belong instead to the type of literature (or genre) that Lewis identified as "sacred fiction."

It is this judgment about literary forms, rather than a lack of confidence in the truthfulness of the Bible, that led Lewis to deny that every sentence of the Old Testament contained historical or scientific truth. "Any more," he said, "than St. Jerome did when he said that Moses described Creation 'after the manner of a popular poet' (as we should say, mythically) or than Calvin did when he doubted whether the story of Job were history or fiction."[39]

Here Lewis reveals his limitations in historical theology, since Calvin never denied the historicity of Job. But what is more important to note is his use of the term *myth* to refer to the early chapters of Genesis and other parts of the Old Testament. This is perhaps the most distinctive and complex dimension of Lewis's views on Scripture. "Of course I believe the composition, presentation, and selection for inclusion in the Bible, of all the books to have been guided by the Holy Ghost," he explained to one of his many correspondents. "But I think He meant us to have sacred myth and sacred fiction as well as sacred history."[40]

What makes this aspect of Lewis's thought so challenging is that he does not use the term *myth* the way most people do. He does not use it the way that Peter used it, for example, when he warned us

---

[38] C. S. Lewis, letter to Janet Wise, October 5, 1955, *Collected Letters, vol. 3*, 652–53.

[39] Lewis, *Reflections on the Psalms*, 92.

[40] Lewis, letter to Janet Wise, *Collected Letters, vol. 3*, 652–53. See also *The Problem of Pain*, where Lewis writes, "I have the deepest respect even for Pagan myths, still more for myths in Holy Scripture" (59).

not to follow "cleverly devised myths" (2 Pet. 1:16). Nor does he use it the way people often use it today, to distinguish history from legend. He does not even use it quite the way that classicists use it to describe the mythology of ancient Greece and Rome. So how *does* he use it?

His Use of "Myth"

For Lewis, myths are stories that awaken the human imagination, embody universal realities, and define the values of a culture. To use Lewis's own terminology, myths are "numinous" and "awe-inspiring." They make us feel "as if something of great moment had been communicated to us."[41] In other words, they bridge the gap between the world of time and space and the eternal realms that lie beyond— much the way that the wardrobe in Professor Kirk's house opened a portal between our own world and the kingdom of Narnia. In bridging this gap, myths allow us "to actually experience Reality and grasp eternal truths."[42]

Nothing in this definition rules out the possibility that mythology may also serve as history. When Lewis uses the word *myth*, he does not mean a story that is not historically true. Rather, he means a story that is rooted in ultimate reality—a story that explains the nature of things and may in fact be true. Some myths are, and some myths are not, grounded in history. So Lewis defined a myth as "an account of what *may have been* the historical fact," which he carefully distinguished from "a symbolical representation of non-historical truth."[43]

When he came to Scripture, Lewis found the main narrative functioning as *both* mythical story and factual history. According to Vanhoozer, "He therefore distinguished himself from fundamentalists, who lost the 'myth' (imagination), and from modern biblical critics, who eliminate the 'became fact' (history)."[44] In fact, as Vanhoozer also points out, Lewis's major criticism of both fundamentalists and

---

[41] C. S. Lewis, *An Experiment in Criticism* (Cambridge, UK: Cambridge University Press, 1961), 44.
[42] Christensen, *C. S. Lewis on Scripture*, 64.
[43] Lewis, *The Problem of Pain*, 64n.
[44] Vanhoozer, "On scripture," 76.

modernists was nearly the same: neither group displayed good literary sense.[45]

In using the term *myth*, Lewis recognized that he was susceptible to misunderstanding. "I must either use the word *myth* or coin a word," he wrote, "and I think the former the lesser evil of the two."[46] He was well aware, for example, that Rudolf Bultmann had been using the term *myth* to attack almost everything in Christianity, up to and including the resurrection of Jesus Christ. Lewis could not have disagreed more. Whereas "for Bultmann, 'myth' was a form of precritical thinking which was no longer viable in the modern world; for Lewis it was an essential form of communication, belonging ineradicably to divinely created human nature as such."[47]

To understand why myth was so important to C. S. Lewis, it helps to know the role that it played in his coming to faith in Jesus Christ. Lewis had loved mythology from early childhood, and gradually he came to realize that the stories that awakened his imagination were pointing him to the truth of the gospel.

In his earlier years, Lewis had described myths as "lies breathed through silver."[48] But a different view began to crystallize for him one day when he was in the Senior Common Room of Magdalene College at the University of Oxford. His colleague T. D. Weldon—the "hardest boiled" of all the atheists that Lewis ever knew—looked up from his reading and said casually, "All that stuff of Frazer's about the Dying God. Rum thing. It almost looks as if it had really happened once."[49] Weldon was referring to the historical evidence for the death and resurrection of Jesus of Nazareth. His comment startled Lewis and sent him back to the Gospels, where he found the true story of a dying and rising deity. Later, Lewis looked back on his conversion and explained how mythology prepared him for the gospel:

---

[45] Ibid., 77.

[46] Lewis, *Experiment in Criticism*, 43.

[47] Alasdair I. C. Heron, "What Is Wrong with Biblical Exegesis?: Reflections upon C. S. Lewis' Criticisms," in *Different Gospels*, ed. Andrew Walker (Kent, UK: Hodder & Stoughton, 1988), 126.

[48] Ibid., 122.

[49] C. S. Lewis, *Surprised by Joy: The Shape of My Early Life* (New York: Harcourt, Brace & Jovanovich, 1955), 211.

If ever a myth had become fact, had been incarnated, it would be just like this. And nothing else in all literature was just like this. Myths were like it in one way. Histories were like it in another. But nothing was simply like it. And no person was like the Person it depicted. . . . Here and here only in all time the myth must have become fact; the Word, flesh; God, Man. This is not "a religion," nor "a philosophy." It is the summing up and actuality of them all.[50]

We hear echoes of this experience in Lewis's famous essay "Myth Become Fact," in which he explains how in world literature "we pass from a Balder or Osiris, dying nobody knows when or where, to a historical Person crucified . . . under Pontius Pilate. . . . The heart of Christianity is a myth which is also a fact. . . . The old myth of the Dying God, *without ceasing to be myth*, comes down from the heaven of legend and imagination to the earth of history. . . . To be truly Christian, we must both assent to the historical fact and also receive the myth (fact though it has become) with the same imaginative embrace we accord to all myths."[51]

The path that Lewis followed in his own spiritual pilgrimage— the path from myth as myth to "myth become fact"—mirrors the progression that he saw at work in Holy Scripture. "The Old Testament contains myth," Lewis wrote, "but it is revelation that comes still more into focus as it goes on. Jonah and the Whale, Noah and his Ark, are fabulous; but the Court history of King David is probably as reliable as the Court History of Louis XIV. Then, in the New Testament, the thing really happens. The dying God really appears—as a historical Person, living in a definite place and time."[52]

Although Lewis was not dogmatic about this theory of progressive revelation, it was the view that he long held. Consider this summary from his book on miracles:

---

[50] Ibid., 88.
[51] C. S. Lewis, *God in the Dock: Essays on Theology and Ethics*, ed. Walter Hooper (Grand Rapids, MI: Eerdmans, 1970), 66–67 (emphasis original).
[52] Lewis, *Surprised by Joy*, 222.

My present view—which is tentative and liable to any amount of correction—would be that just as, on the factual side, a long preparation culminates in God's becoming incarnate as Man, so, on the documentary side, the truth first appears in *mythical* form and then by a long process of condensing or focusing finally becomes incarnate as History. This involves the belief that Myth in general is not merely misunderstood history . . . nor diabolical illusion . . . nor priestly lying . . . but, at its best, a real though unfocused gleam of divine truth falling on human imagination.[53]

The process that Lewis describes was something that God intended; it was all under his sovereign control. Lewis wrote,

The Hebrews, like other people, had mythology: but as they were the chosen people so their mythology was the chosen mythology—the mythology chosen by God to be the vehicle of the earliest sacred truth, the first step in that process which ends in the New Testament where truth has become completely historical. Whether we can say with certainty where, in this process of crystallization, any particular Old Testament story falls, is another matter. I take it that the memoirs of David's court come at one end of the scale and are scarcely less historical than St. Mark or Acts; and that the Book of Jonah is at the opposite end.[54]

So far, we have considered two main qualifications to Lewis's views on the inspiration and authority of Holy Scripture. The first is that he was not a theologian, and he knew it, so he was careful not to present a definitive doctrine of Scripture. The second is that in regarding certain parts of the Bible as mythical or fictional, he was not necessarily denying their historicity. For Lewis, myth had become fact.

---

[53] C. S. Lewis, *Miracles: A Preliminary Study* (New York: Macmillan, 1947), 161n1 (emphasis original).
[54] Ibid. Lewis also wrote, "If you take the Bible as a whole, you see a process in which something which, in its earliest levels . . . was hardly moral at all, and was in some ways not unlike the Pagan religions, is gradually purged and enlightened till it becomes the religion of the great prophets of Our Lord Himself. That whole process is the greatest revelation of God's true nature." Letter to Mrs. Johnson, May 14, 1955, *Collected Letters, vol. 3*, 608.

Rarely Affecting His Theology as a Whole

A third qualification to make, very briefly, is that *whatever deficiencies we find in Lewis's doctrine of Scripture rarely seem to affect his theology as a whole.* Typically, theologians who have anything less than the highest view of Scripture downgrade other doctrines as well. They back away from the hard sayings of Jesus, for example, or become skeptical about biblical miracles, or dismiss the deity of Christ.

Yet C. S. Lewis continued to give a robust defense of biblical Christianity. Possibly this is because, like most principled Anglicans, he was thoroughly committed to the creeds of Christendom that ran from the early church right up through the Reformation, including the Thirty-Nine Articles. Or perhaps Lewis stayed within the boundaries of orthodoxy because, whatever doubts he may have held about the Old Testament, he was completely convinced that the Gospels give us the true words of Jesus Christ.[55]

Some Strengths

There is another possible explanation, however: despite his demurrals on inerrancy, Lewis generally had a high view of Scripture, not a low one. This brings us, finally, to some of the strengths in his understanding and use of the Bible.

Given the cloud of suspicion that surrounds Lewis's doctrine of Scripture, we should be careful not to miss the constructive dimensions of his approach to the Bible. In considering these strengths, we need not minimize the real problems in his views on inspiration and inerrancy, but we should also learn what we can from the way Lewis read the Bible and defended it against the attacks of unbelievers.

His Doctrine Surrendered to Scripture

To begin, C. S. Lewis believed that *Christian doctrine should always be surrendered to Scripture.* As we have seen, he had a healthy respect for theological tradition, as codified in the creeds of the church. But

---

[55] Garry Friesen makes both of these points in his essay "Scripture in the Writings of C. S. Lewis."

his theological norm was the Bible, which he typically referred to as "Holy Scripture." If we believe that God has spoken, Lewis wrote in a letter to the editor of *Theology*, naturally we will "listen to what He has to say."[56] In his personal letters, Lewis urged his friends and other correspondents to follow this principle and submit to biblical authority. Here are a few examples:

> What we are committed to believing is whatever can be proved from Scripture.[57]

> Yes, Pascal does directly contradict several passages in Scripture and must be wrong.[58]

> I take it as a first principle that we must not interpret any one part of Scripture so that it contradicts other parts.[59]

In giving these exhortations, Lewis took both sides of a doctrinal equation: we believe what the Bible affirms *and* we do not believe what the Bible denies. Furthermore, he insisted on accepting the unity and consistency of the Bible (a view that is in tension with his concern elsewhere that there might be contradictions in the Bible).

We see Lewis applying the principle of letting Scripture interpret Scripture to two of the doctrines he found it hardest to understand. One was the sovereignty of God over human suffering. In a letter offering spiritual counsel he wrote,

> The two things one must NOT do are (a) To believe, on the strength of Scripture or on any other evidence, that God is in any way evil. (In Him is no *darkness* at all.) (b) To wipe off the slate any passage which seems to show that He is. Behind that apparently shocking passage, be sure, there lurks some great truth which you don't understand. If one ever *does* come to understand it, one

---

[56] Lewis, in *Christian Reflections*, 27.
[57] C. S. Lewis, in a 1945 letter to Lyman Stebbins, quoted by James Como, "C. S. Lewis' Quantum Church: An Uneasy Meditation," in *C. S. Lewis and the Church*, 98.
[58] C. S. Lewis, letter to Dom Bede Griffiths, May 28, 1952, *Collected Letters*, vol. 3, 195.
[59] C. S. Lewis, letter to Emily McLay, August 3, 1953, *Collected Letters*, vol. 3, 354.

will see that [He] is good and just and gracious in ways we never dreamed of. Till then, it must be just left on one side.[60]

Another example of Lewis's submission to Holy Scripture is his somewhat reluctant yet strong affirmation of the doctrine of hell, simply on the grounds of biblical authority. In *The Problem of Pain* he wrote, "There is no doctrine which I would more willingly remove from Christianity than this, if it lay in my power. But it has the full support of Scripture and, specially, of Our Lord's own words."[61]

Lewis was far more concerned with what Scripture said than with what the scholars said. When one of his readers—who was tempted to come under the influence of modernist theology—wrote to express her doubts about the virgin birth, Lewis sent her back to Holy Scripture: "*Your* starting point about this doctrine will not, I think, be to collect the opinion of individual clergymen, but to read Matthew Chapter I and Luke I and II."[62]

One can only wish that Lewis had followed this principle a little more closely in developing his theology of Holy Scripture. He never seems to have given serious consideration to the biblical texts in which the Bible speaks to its own inspiration and authority. Perhaps this explains why he never developed a fully biblical doctrine of Scripture: Lewis did not pay close enough attention to what the Bible says about its own nature—the self-understanding of Scripture. At the risk of speculating again, one cannot help but think that he would have had more fully evangelical views on Scripture if he had spent more time reflecting on biblical texts such as 2 Timothy 3:16 and 2 Peter 1:21. Yet the fact remains that C. S. Lewis wanted his doctrine to be derived from Scripture.

His Sensitivity to Literary Genre

Another strength of his approach to Scripture was his *sensitive reading of each biblical text according to its literary form.* Lewis read the Bible

---

[60] Ibid., 356–57 (emphases original).
[61] Lewis, *The Problem of Pain*, 106.
[62] C. S. Lewis, letter to Genia Goelz, June 13, 1959, *Collected Letters, vol. 3*, 127 (emphasis original).

as literature decades before it became fashionable to do so. Not that he read the Bible *merely* as literature, of course. In fact, Lewis was highly critical of any attempt to claim that the Bible had any unique literary majesty apart from its sacred authorship and saving message. "Unless the religious claims of the Bible are again acknowledged," he wrote, "its literary claims will, I think, be given only 'mouth honour' and that decreasingly. For it is, through and through, a sacred book."[63]

In reading the Bible as literature, Lewis was in his element. His primary calling was as an English professor, and in this he was virtually without peer. While at Oxford, he wrote a famous volume on the sixteenth century for the *Oxford History of English Literature*, and in 1954 he was awarded the chair of Mediaeval and Renaissance Literature at Cambridge University.

Lewis thus came to Holy Scripture as a reader, not a theologian—someone for whom the Bible was always more than literature, but could never be less.[64] This is one of the things that he appreciated most about the Bible, both as a Christian and as a literary critic: in the Bible a variety of literary forms—chronicles, poems, moral and political diatribes, romances, and what have you—have been "taken into the service of God's word."[65]

Naturally, Lewis insisted on reading every part of the Bible according to its genre. Because the Bible is literature, it "cannot properly be read except as literature; and the different parts of it as the different sorts of literature they are."[66] There are even different kinds of narrative—and it would be illogical to read them all in the same way.[67] One has to take the Bible for what it is, Lewis insisted, and it "demands incessantly to be taken on its own terms."[68]

Not everyone will agree with all of Lewis's literary judgments.

---

[63] C. S. Lewis, *The Literary Impact of the Authorized Version* (Philadelphia: Fortress, 1963), 32.
[64] Vanhoozer, "On scripture," 76.
[65] Lewis, *Reflections on the Psalms*, 111.
[66] Ibid., 3.
[67] Lewis, letter to Carnell, *Collected Letters, vol. 3*, 319.
[68] Lewis, *Literary Impact*, 97.

Jonah is a notable example. Lewis did not doubt the book's historicity because he denied that there was a fish big enough to swallow a
man, or because he had scientific reasons for thinking that no prophet
could survive for three days in the belly of a whale. He reached this
conclusion because, he said, "the whole *Book of Jonah* has to me the air
of being a moral romance, a quite different *kind* of thing from, say, the
account of King David or the New Testament narratives, not *pegged*,
like them, into any historical situation."[69]

Although Jonah's prophecy referred to real places, it was not tied
in to historical chronology like Kings or Chronicles. Lewis did not
therefore believe that Jonah was historically false; rather, he believed
that it never presented itself as history at all. Strictly speaking, he
never denied the inerrancy of Jonah but took an alternative view of
its literary genre.

Most evangelicals believe that Lewis was mistaken. However,
the way to convince him of this mistake would not have been by
defending some a priori doctrine of biblical inerrancy. Instead, one
would have to persuade him that the Bible did in fact present Jonah
as history—an argument one might make from literary qualities of
the book itself and from references to the prophet in the Old and New
Testaments.

When it came to many other books of the Bible—particularly
in the New Testament—Lewis insisted that they be read as history.
Here we see the strength of his attention to genre. In one essay,
he criticized Bible scholars who regarded the Gospel of John as
a poetic, spiritual "romance," rather than as historical narrative.
Lewis frankly doubted that such scholars knew very much about
literature at all. "I have been reading poems, romances, vision-
literature, legends, myths all my life," he wrote. "I know what they
are like." So if someone "tells me that something in a Gospel is
legend or romance," he wrote, "I want to know how many legends
and romances he has read, how well his palate is trained in detect-

---

[69] Lewis, letter to Carnell, *Collected Letters, vol. 3*, 319 (emphasis original).

ing them by the flavor; not how many years he has spent on that Gospel."[70]

For his own part, Lewis had little doubt that the Gospel of John was reliable history. "Either this is reportage," he wrote "though it may no doubt contain errors—pretty close up to the facts; nearly as close as Boswell. Or else [and here Lewis is writing entirely tongue-in-cheek], some unknown writer in the second century, without known predecessors or successors, suddenly anticipated the whole technique of modern, novelistic, realistic, narrative."[71]

C. S. Lewis generally found critical Bible scholars "to lack literary judgment, to be imperceptive about the very quality of the texts they are reading."[72] He admitted that this was "a strange charge to bring against men who have been steeped in those books all their lives." "But that might be just the trouble," he wrote: "A man who has spent his youth and manhood in the minute study of New Testament texts and of other people's studies of them, whose literary experience of those texts lacks any standard of comparison such as can only grow from a wide and deep and genial experience of literature in general, is . . . very likely to miss the obvious things about them."[73]

To use the analogy that Lewis gave, these scholars "claim to see fern-seed and can't see an elephant ten yards away in broad daylight." They "ask me to believe they can read between the lines of the old texts; the evidence is their obvious inability to read (in any sense worth discussing) the lines themselves."[74]

His Commitment to the Biblical Miracles

In defending John and the other Gospels against their critics, C. S. Lewis was *steadfastly committed to the historicity and validity of biblical miracles*—another strength of his reading of Scripture. He not only believed in miracles but also defended them against their critics. In

---

[70] Lewis, "Modern Theology," 154–55.
[71] Ibid., 155.
[72] Ibid., 154.
[73] Ibid.
[74] Ibid., 157.

fact, Lewis saw this as the bright line that divided authentic Christianity from all its pretenders. He wrote, "To me the real distinction is . . . between religion with a real supernaturalism and salvationism on the one hand, and all watered-down and modernist versions on the other."[75]

What marked the dividing line for Lewis were the biblical miracles: "They are recorded as events on this earth which affected human senses. They are the sort of thing we can describe literally. If Christ turned water into wine, and we had been present, we could have seen, smelled, and tasted. . . . It is either fact, or legend, or lie. You must take it or leave it."[76] Readers who are familiar with the "Lord, liar, or lunatic" *tri-lemma* that Lewis posed in *Mere Christianity* have encountered this type of apologetic reasoning before. When it came to miracles, including the miracle of the incarnation, it was all or nothing for Lewis.

What was not an option, as far as Lewis was concerned, was to rule out the very possibility of miracles the way that modern, supposedly scientific scholars tended to do. Here is what he wrote in *Fern-seed and Elephants* about biblical scholarship that denied the miraculous:

> Scholars, as scholars, speak on [this question] with no more authority than anyone else. The canon "If miraculous, unhistorical" is one they bring to their study of texts, not one they have learned from it. If one is speaking of authority, the united authority of all the Biblical critics in the world counts here for nothing. On this they speak simply as men; men obviously influenced by, and perhaps insufficiently critical of, the spirit of the age they grew up in.[77]

His Anti-Liberal Views on Scripture

It was because he believed in miracles—including, supremely, the miraculous resurrection of Jesus Christ—that Lewis was so critical

---

[75] C. S. Lewis, letter to Sister Penelope, November 8, 1939, *Collected Letters*, vol. 2, 285.
[76] C. S. Lewis, "Horrid Red Things," in *God in the Dock*, 71.
[77] Lewis, "Modern Theology," 158.

of liberal scholarship on the Bible. Here we can make explicit a point that more or less has been made already: *C. S. Lewis was anti-liberal in his views on Holy Scripture.* While we may be critical of him for failing in various ways to espouse a fully biblical doctrine of Scripture, it is only fair to say that he spent far more time defending the Bible than he did criticizing it, which he hardly did at all.

C. S. Lewis was so anti-liberal that many of his contemporaries labeled him as a fundamentalist. Here is how he explained their attitude toward his theology:

> I have been suspected of being what is called a Fundamentalist. That is because I never regard any narrative as unhistorical simply on the ground that it includes the miraculous. Some people find the miraculous so hard to believe that they cannot imagine any reason for my acceptance of it other than a prior belief that every sentence of the Old Testament has historical or scientific truth. But this I do not hold.[78]

Needless to say, Lewis's defense of miracles led many liberal scholars to treat him with suspicion. For his own part, Lewis regarded liberal scholars as wolves among the sheep, especially "the divines engaged in New Testament criticism," whom he held chiefly responsible for undermining theological orthodoxy.[79]

Lewis exacted his revenge in the fiction he wrote. *The Screwtape Letters; That Hideous Strength;* and *The Great Divorce* all feature liberal clergy who are held up to mockery. Lewis treated them this way because he believed that liberal Christianity was not real Christianity at all. Instead, it was "a theology which denies the historicity of nearly everything in the Gospels to which Christian life and affections and thought have been fastened for nearly two millennia—which either denies the miraculous altogether or, more strangely, after swallowing the camel of the Resurrection strains at such gnats as the feeding of the multitudes."[80]

[78] Lewis, *Reflections on the Psalms*, 109.
[79] Lewis, "Modern Theology," 153.
[80] Ibid.

Lewis proceeded to explain what happens when this kind of Christianity, so-called, is offered to an ordinary person who has recently come to faith in Christ. Either the convert will leave a liberal church and find one where biblical Christianity is actually taught, or else eventually he will leave Christianity altogether. "If he agrees with your version [of the Christian faith]," Lewis said to his liberal opponents, "he will no longer call himself a Christian and no longer come to church."[81] Lewis made a similar point in *Letters to Malcolm* by asking a rhetorical question: "By the way, did you ever meet, or hear of, anyone who was converted from skepticism to a 'liberal' or 'de-mythologized' Christianity?" Lewis never had, which led him to claim "that when unbelievers come in at all, they come in a good deal further."[82] What he meant by "a good deal further" was authentic faith in the risen Lord Jesus Christ.

The place where Lewis learned the difference between authentic and inauthentic faith was in the Scriptures of the Old and New Testaments, which he believed to be the very word of God. Vanhoozer aptly concludes that Lewis "occupies that sparse territory between fundamentalists and modern critics that is contiguous to but does not coincide with Evangelicalism."[83] Perhaps we could go further and say that Lewis's doctrine of Scripture is not merely adjacent to but often overlaps with evangelical theology. One area where evangelicals surely agree with Lewis in his views is that we should read Holy Scripture on its own terms, fully submitting to its authority, and completely surrendering to God's will for our lives—lest, like Jill Pole and Eustace Scrubb, we miss the signs and lose our way.

---

[81] Ibid.
[82] C. S. Lewis, *Letters to Malcolm: Chiefly on Prayer* (London: Geoffrey Bles, 1964), 152–53.
[83] Vanhoozer, "On scripture," 82.

3

UNDRAGONED

C. S. Lewis on the Gift of Salvation

DOUGLAS WILSON

It would be easy to represent what I am about to attempt here as part of an unseemly struggle over the body of Moses. Everybody wants a piece of Lewis—right?—and so here come the Reformed, late to the game, hindered in this particular footrace by the ball and chain of predestination. I would get rid of it, but I can't help it.

Now, I don't want to be a participant in *any* unseemly struggles, retroactively claiming somebody for "our side," that somebody being now deceased. I don't want to do that with anybody, much less over the venerable Lewis. I am reminded of what Lewis himself said in another context about the assured results of modern scholarship concerning the past—that they were only assured results because the men involved were dead and couldn't blow the gaff.

So let me begin by noting what I am *not* seeking to do. I am not trying to represent Lewis as a doctrinaire five-pointer, or as someone in the grip of any precise system whatever. He was a churchman—not a party man, not a faction member. This disclaimer even includes the true system of doctrine that, as we all know, the archangel Gabriel delivered in 1619 to the Synod of Dort.

At the same time—and you should have known a qualification was coming—I do want to maintain that Lewis had a firm grasp of

is he Calvinist
(protestant)
v iew of salvation

the true *graciousness* of saving grace, and that he knew that a recovery of this understanding was an essential part of the rise of classical Protestantism. In this chapter, I hope that you will see Lewis as at *least* a sympathetic observer of historic Reformation theology, or—at most—an asystematic adherent of it. This latter position is the position I hold. So was C. S. Lewis small-*r* reformed? Not exactly, and yes, of course.

Keep in mind that Lewis's thought developed over time. I am drawing largely from his *English Literature in the Sixteenth Century*, which was his magnum opus, a product of his mature thought. And while Tolkien and Lewis were lifelong friends, their friendship was strained in the latter years. Tolkien was a devout Roman Catholic, and he saw this book as an example of Lewis returning to his Belfast roots.

One other quick point should be made at the outset concerning my qualifications even to talk about this. Am *I* Reformed? Am *I* a Calvinist? This is a point upon which I understand there has been some discussion. Well, in brief, I wish there were seven points so I could hold to the Calvinistic extras. You may count me a devotee of crawl-over-broken-glass Calvinism, jet-fuel Calvinism, black-coffee Calvinism. Or, as my friend Peter Hitchens had it, weapons-grade Calvinism. No yellowcake uranium semi-Pelagianism for me. I buy my Calvinism in fifty-gallon drums with the skull and crossbones stenciled on the side, with little dribbles of white paint running down from the corners. I get my Calvinism delivered on those forklift plats at Costco. I trust this reassures everyone, and I am glad we had this little chat.

Asystematic? Or Just Muddled?

It doesn't happen very often, but when it does, C. S. Lewis is perhaps the most insightful muddler you will ever read. He, along with Chesterton, has the capacity to edify you profoundly at the very moment he is saying things to make you wrench at your head in exasperation. I am thinking here of a book such as *Reflections on the Psalms*.

But when he is on, which is almost always, you can be done with the wrenching and just enjoy the edification. So there's that.

Having said this, in *The Screwtape Letters* Lewis takes a jab at modern man, who is accustomed to carrying around a mass of contradictions: "Your man has been accustomed, ever since he was a boy, to having a dozen incompatible philosophies dancing about together in his head."[1] And Owen Barfield once said that Lewis himself was utterly *unlike* this, saying that what Lewis thought about everything was contained in what he said about anything.

I add this because I believe that there are many times when we are wrenching at our heads in exasperation over Lewis while the heavenly host is looking down on *us*, wrenching at their heads—if angels do that. There will be times when we are tempted to write off something in Lewis as a simple contradiction, when *we* are the ones who have not thought very deeply about what we are saying. Michael Ward has shown in *Planet Narnia* that Lewis could look like he was just dashing something off when he was actually building an impressive structure on deep foundations. So let us feel free to differ with him, but let's also take care not to be patronizing.

Make no mistake, Lewis had an intentional project, and that project is still a gathering river, one which shows no sign of diminishing. It is already astonishingly wide, and it is only down as far as Vicksburg. We ought not to be patronizing in how we "forgive" Lewis's little side ventures and do some more serious thinking about how he managed to pull off something like this massive project.

Peter Escalante has argued—in an outstanding presentation on Italian humanism and *its* cultural impact, represented by men like Dante—the following:

> Can any of you think of outstanding examples in our own time of the Italian humanist style? Let me give a checklist: 1) a trained philologist devoted to comprehensive Christian wisdom, 2) exploring and expressing the themes of that wisdom in widely

---

[1] C. S. Lewis, *The Screwtape Letters* (New York: Macmillan, 1962), 8.

various literary genres and for a while abstaining from formal systematic presentation, 3) addressing the general public rather than a professional elite, 4) passionately concerned about the whole commonwealth, and 5) with a vision of the cosmos which has *poiesis* as its very heart?[2]

Right. The answer is C. S. Lewis.

His Own Experience

With all of this said, in what might *appear* to be a somewhat desultory beginning, I think we should all exhort me to pull it together and try to bring in some razor-sharp focus. So let's begin our discussion of Lewis's view of salvation by looking at Lewis's view of his *own* salvation.

The whole issue really boils down to how you understand the grace of God. Is salvation a cooperative affair, or does God simply intervene to bless us by taking the initiative? Was Lazarus raised from the dead in a semi-Pelagian fashion, with Lazarus pushing and Jesus pulling, or not?

Watch C. S. Lewis describe a moment in his own conversion:

> In a sense I was not moved by anything. I chose to open, to un-buckle, to loosen the rein. I say "I chose," *yet it did not really seem possible to do the opposite.* On the other hand, I was aware of no motives. You could argue that I was not a free agent, but I am more inclined to think that this came nearer to being a perfectly free act than most that I have ever done. *Necessity may not be the opposite of freedom,* and perhaps a man is most free when, instead of producing motives, he could only say, "I am what I do."[3]

As Ransom discovered on Perelandra, freedom and necessity are actually the same thing. Lewis had this to say about freedom and

---

[2] Personal communication to the author.
[3] C. S. Lewis, *Surprised by Joy: The Shape of My Early Life* (New York: Harcourt, Brace & World, 1955), 224–25 (emphases added).

grace: "When we carry it up to relations between God and Man, has the distinction perhaps become nonsensical? After all, when we are most free, it is only with a freedom God has given us: and when our will is most influenced by Grace, it is still our will."[4]

Moving to the experience of conversion as it was experienced by others, Lewis describes the experience of conversion as it was felt by "an early Protestant."[5] He says this: "All the initiative has been on God's side; all has been free, unbounded grace. And all will continue to be free, unbounded grace."[6] He is clearly in sympathy with this, for this is how *he* experienced it.

Can't Tell the Players without a Scorecard

Now if we want to pursue this discussion, keep in mind that terms do not always stay put in history. When we refer to Calvinism today, we are usually talking about soteriology—the five points. Thus it is that a man can be a Calvinist and also be a dispensationalist, a charismatic, or even a Presbyterian. That last has been known to happen. I've met some.

But during the reigns of Elizabeth I and James I, identifying as a Calvinist was more about *ecclesiology*, including your view of the sacraments. In this sense, a bunch of the non-Calvinists (their sense) were all Calvinists (our sense). One of the historiographical fiascos caused by the Oxford Movement happened as the result of their vain attempt to pretend that the Church of England was not part of the Continental Reformed community of churches—but it *manifestly* was.

Lewis was a conservative Anglican churchman, who understood the Thirty-Nine Articles in their original context, and *they* were robustly Calvinistic. He was thoroughly sympathetic with theologians such as Hooker, Jewel, or Andrews who were not exactly Victorian Anglo-Catholics. They were *Protestants*, and Calvinists in a broad sense. They were a key part of the Reformed churches of Europe,

[4] C. S. Lewis, *Yours, Jack*, 1st ed. (New York: HarperOne, 2008), 186
[5] C. S. Lewis, *English Literature in the Sixteenth Century* (London: Oxford University Press, 1954), 33.
[6] Ibid., 34.

position of balance + peace among factions

which is exactly where they wanted to be. Lewis, as a literary historian, knew what they were teaching, and he identified with them. But
as a natural-born irenicist, he also wanted to keep the peace for the
sake of *contemporary* inter-Anglican affairs. This meant that the *precise*
historical nature of the founding of the Church of England sometimes
got a bit blurred. But even with that said, Lewis is far more helpful
on this period than many who ought to know better.

Speaking of ecclesiology, remember the vivid picture of the
church "spread out through all time and space and rooted in eternity,
terrible as an army with banners."[7] And also remember that Lewis's
most famous phrase—mere Christianity—is taken from Baxter. This
is plainly Protestant ecclesiology. Some staunch Protestants may be
distressed by the fact that, at the beginning of *Mere Christianity*, Lewis
grants the Roman Catholics a "room" in the great house of our faith,
wondering why the Catholics get a room. But we shouldn't forget
that this conception of the house is a *Protestant* conception.

Some Citations

Now, there are places where Lewis is critical of the Calvinists and the
Puritan party in England,[8] but there are other places where he praises
them earnestly. He refers to "the whole tragic farce which we call the
history of the Reformation."[9] Here is his snapshot description of some
of the historical theology of that day:

> In fact, however, these questions [about faith and works] were
> raised at a moment when they immediately became embittered
> and entangled with a whole complex of matters theologically ir-
> relevant, and therefore attracted the fatal attention of both gov-
> ernment and the mob. . . . It was as if men were set to conduct a
> metaphysical argument at a fair, in competition or (worse still)
> forced collaboration with the cheapjacks and the round-abouts,

---

[7] Lewis, *Screwtape Letters*, 12.
[8] E.g., Lewis, *English Literature*, 49.
[9] Ibid., 37.

indulgences etc.

under the eyes of an armed and vigilant police force who frequently changed sides.[10]

With his sympathies established, let me turn to a sample citation that seems to contradict the notion that Lewis could in any way be considered Reformed. Speaking of total depravity, he says, "I disbelieve that doctrine, partly on the logical ground that if our depravity were total we should not know ourselves to be depraved, and partly because experience shows us much goodness in human nature."[11] But of course, in this he is actually rejecting a doctrine of *absolute* depravity, which not one of us holds. But if total depravity means total inability, which it does, it would be the work of ten minutes to show that Lewis does in fact hold to it—as we shall see in a moment.

In these sorts of formal rejections, Lewis follows his teacher Chesterton. And even Chesterton, who takes shots at Calvinism every third chance he gets, cannot stay out of the truth. For example, in *Orthodoxy* Chesterton writes, "Thus he has always believed there is such a thing as fate, but such a thing as free will also." Well, hey, and amen.

But the key to this is a series of statements in which Lewis acknowledges that the classical Protestant position was actually in some fashion a reiteration of the Pauline teaching. Look for that key word *Pauline*. Lewis uses it repeatedly in this context: under certain calm conditions, "formulae might possibly have been found which did justice to the Protestant—*I had almost said Pauline*—assertions without compromising other elements of the Christian faith."[12]

In a letter to a Mrs. Emily McLay, he uses an illustration from quantum physics:

> I take it as a first principle that we must not interpret any one part of Scripture so that it contradicts other parts. . . . The real inter-relation between God's omnipotence and Man's freedom is something we can't find out. Looking at the Sheep and the Goats

[10] Ibid.

[11] C. S. Lewis, *The Problem of Pain* (New York: Macmillan, 1962), 66.

[12] Lewis, *English Literature*, 37 (emphasis added).

every man can be quite sure that every kind act he does will be accepted by Christ. Yet, equally, we all do feel sure that all the good in us comes from Grace. We have to leave it at that. I find the best plan is to take the Calvinist view of my own virtues and other people's vices; and the other view of my own vices and other people's virtues. But tho' there is much to be puzzled about, there is nothing to be *worried* about. It is plain from Scripture that, *in whatever sense the Pauline doctrine is true*, it is not true in any sense which excludes its (apparent) opposite. You know what Luther said: "Do you doubt if you are chosen? Then say your prayers and you may conclude that you are."[13]

Notice him citing *Luther* there.

Lewis held that the Pauline (Protestant) doctrine is obviously true in *some* sense but that we ought not to throw out other truths for the sake of our system. Again, amen.

And in this following citation, he thinks he has not tipped his hand, but I am afraid he has. "Theologically, Protestantism was either a recovery, or a development, or an exaggeration (it is not for the literary historian to say which) *of Pauline theology.*"[14]

Lewis plainly does not believe in the Calvinistic caricatures, but neither do we. And when he speaks in his own voice, he says things that themselves are susceptible to the same sort of caricature: "You will certainly carry out God's purpose, but it makes a difference to you whether you serve like Judas or like John."[15]

Undragoned

Let me take a moment to conduct a very brief tour of the Narnian tulip garden—a place of fond memories for me because this is where I first learned my foundational lessons in the meaning of grace. Now I admit that these are *Narnian* tulips, so they don't look quite the same

---

[13] C. S. Lewis, *The Collected Letters of C. S. Lewis, vol. 3: Narnia, Cambridge, and Joy, 1950–1963*, ed. Walter Hooper (San Francisco: HarperSanFrancisco, 2007), 354–55 (latter emphasis added).
[14] Lewis, *English Literature*, 33 (emphasis added).
[15] Lewis, *The Problem of Pain*, 111.

as what we are used to—they are larger, for one, and they open to the sun more quickly than those that some of our stricter brethren have duct-taped shut. Nevertheless, we should be able to quickly recognize the gaudy splash of colors that characterize our floral theology. It is either the Calvinist tulip or the Arminian daisy—"He loves me, He loves me not . . ." *raised in Atheism*

unpleasant boy—
Eustace was miserable as a dragon and discovered that he was utterly unable to heal himself or prepare himself to be healed. When he tried to remove the dragon skin by himself, all he was able to do was get down underneath his dragon skin—to the *next* layer of dragon skin. And you know while you are reading this passage, beyond any shadow of any doubt, that as long as Eustace was doing his *own* scraping, it would be dragon skins all the way down.

When Peter, Susan, Edmund, and Lucy arrive in Narnia for the first time, they discover—among many other things—that four thrones were empty at Cair Paravel, empty and waiting for them. Not only that; there were prophecies about them. And in a later book, when Jill tries to explain to Aslan that they had called on him, he replies that if he had not called them, they would not have called him. The initiative is all his. "'You would not have called to me unless I had been calling to you,' said the Lion."[16]

When Aslan is killed on the Stone Table, it is for one person—the traitor Edmund. The great lion gave his life for one grimy, little boy. Now it is true that Tirian in *The Last Battle* says that it was by Aslan's blood that all Narnia was saved, but while glorious, this is an application, an extension, an afterthought. The nature of the lion's death as told in the foundational story is seen as a very definite atonement. *Jesus died for us*
It really has to be—Lewis held to substitutionary atonement, and as Garry Williams has clearly shown in *From Heaven He Came and Sought Her*, the two doctrines are logically intertwined.[17] He who says A may not have said B, but give him time.

---

[16] C. S. Lewis, *The Silver Chair* (New York: HarperCollins, 1953), 24–25.

[17] Garry Williams, "The Definite Intent of Penal Substitutionary Atonement," in *From Heaven He Came and Sought Her*, ed. David Gibson and Jonathan Gibson (Wheaton, IL: Crossway, 2013).

When Jill encounters Aslan in his high country, he is between her and the stream. The stream is living water, and she is nearly frantic for it. She is invited to drink, but the lion is in between. She asks if he could go away while she drinks, and is answered with a very low growl. She asks if he will promise not to do anything to her if she does come. "I make no promise," Aslan said. She then asks if he eats girls. "'I have swallowed up girls and boys, women and men, kings and emperors, cities and realms,' said the Lion."

She says she "daren't come and drink." "'Then you will die of thirst,' said the Lion." She resolves to go and look for another stream. "'There is no other stream,' said the Lion."

Now notice how Lewis brings this glorious tension to a close and how much like his description of his own conversion it seems—"and her mind suddenly made itself up."[18]

If this is semi-Pelagianism, then semi-Pelagianism has sure come a long way since I was stuck in it. This ain't your grandma's semi-Pelagianism.

When it comes to perseverance, many of us might think instantly of Susan. Is she not missing from that glorious reunion in *The Last Battle*?[19] But I submit that this is a simple mistake. Susan was not killed in that last railway accident, and we shouldn't speculate about her final destiny unless we want Aslan to growl at us for impudent guesswork about someone else's story. And besides, if anybody wants to argue that the ultimate Cair Paravel in the center of the ultimate Narnia only had three thrones in it, well, I wish them luck. Bless me, it's all in the *Institutes*—bless me, what do they teach them in these schools?

The Buoyancy of Grace

Lewis plainly understands the *relief* that real grace provides. One of the most compelling factors in this discussion, for me, is the fact that Lewis plainly knows how salvation *tastes*:

---

[18] Lewis, *The Silver Chair*, 23.
[19] C. S. Lewis, *The Last Battle* (New York: HarperCollins, 1956), 154.

From this buoyant humility, this farewell to the self with all its good resolutions, anxiety, scruples, and motive scratchings, *all the Protestant doctrines originally sprang.* For it must be clearly understood that they were at first doctrines not of terror but of joy and hope: indeed, more than hope, fruition, for as Tyndale says, the converted man is already tasting eternal life. The doctrine of predestination, says the Seventeenth Article, is "full of sweet, pleasant and unspeakable comfort to godly persons." . . . Relief and buoyancy are the characteristic notes.[20]

That's how it tastes. So how does it taste in a story?

Story Always Wins

Writing a story involves high theology, and the good ones involve the kind of high theology we have been dealing with here. It may not seem like that, but there are many theological assumptions that have to go into a rollicking good yarn. Great writers will have reflected on the reality of this, and great Christian writers tie those reflections in with what God has revealed to us about the story *he* is telling.

There are so many directions we can take with this—and we really ought to spend the rest of our lives taking them all. Storytelling is tied in with the Trinity, with the doctrine of creation, with the incarnation, with death and resurrection, and with the great denouement of the eschaton—or to use Tolkien's great word, the final eucatastrophe.

How could we *not* be storytellers? We worship God the writer, God the written, and God the reader. How could we not create? We are created in God's image, and *he* creates. He created us so that we would do this. He came down into our world to show us how it is done; his name is Immanuel. God loves cliffhangers. He loves nailbiters. On the mount of the Lord it will be provided. Exile and return stories are everywhere. So are death and resurrection stories. So are the-elder-shall-serve-the-younger stories. And the whole thing

---

[20] Lewis, *English Literature*, 33–34 (emphasis added).

will come together at the last day, as promised in Romans 8:28, with trillions of plot points all resolved and no remainder. And the great throng gathered before the throne will cry out, with a voice like many waters, saying, "*That* was the best story we ever heard."

Only God creates ex nihilo. He speaks, and the cosmos springs from nothing. When we create, we are fashioning or reassembling. A carpenter works with wood, a musician with notes, an author with words. All of our material is part of the a priori givenness of creation. When Tolkien spoke of our storytelling as sub-creation, he acknowledged that we create from preexisting materials—we are not God.

But if we are imitating him rightly, we are still imitating an ex nihilo creation. We are reaching for something that is out of our reach—which can be either arrogant or humble, depending on whether or not we were told to reach for it.

A creature cannot imitate the Creator, and yet this is precisely what we are told to do (Eph. 5:1). Earlier in Ephesians, Paul was praying that the saints would be able to comprehend things such as "breadth and length and height, and depth" (Eph. 3:18). He wanted them to know what couldn't be known (Eph. 3:19), speaking of the love of Christ. He wanted them to be filled with all the fullness of God (Eph. 3:19), which is like wanting the Pacific Ocean in your little thimble. *Think* of it.

For reasons having to do with his good pleasure, God has put eternity in our hearts. This is why we cannot find out what God has done, and this is also one of the ways that we are used by him to make everything beautiful in its time. "He has made everything beautiful in its time. Also, he has put eternity into man's heart, yet so that he cannot find out what God has done from the beginning to the end" (Eccles. 3:11).

Hack writers do not sub-create a world; they simply rearrange furniture in a glibly assumed (and largely unexamined) prefab world. If necessary, they make it an "other world" fantasy by hanging two moons in the sky or by naming their protagonist something like Shambilar. But this is just moving things around on the surface. There is no deep structure to it—the author is not exercising enough authority. He is being too timid. There is not enough deep structure because there is not enough deep imitation.

Michael Ward has cogently argued that one of the things that made Lewis's fiction so compelling was the element of "donegality" in it, the ability to make a place really *feel* like that place. The name came from an observation Lewis had made about the "feel" of County Donegal in Ireland. It is the reason why Narnia *tastes* the way it does. And yet Lewis accomplished this by imitating the discarded image, the medieval model of the entire solar system. He went big.

If you try to create a place by simply attaching a label to it, a label that says something like "Narnia," the result will be listless, flat. If you establish the donegality through deep imitation, that atmosphere can even swallow up things that don't rightly belong there—like Mrs. Beaver's sewing machine. The problem is not the use of tools but the use of tools that presuppose industrialization. But because of the donegality, this is scarcely noticed.

That imitation will be of the triune God, of the flow of redemptive-historical theology, of Israel cascading out of Egypt, of the Lord battering down the gates of Hades. You must know—going into it—that nothing you imitate can fit in your word count. But it *will* be a world your word count can fit into.

Several other points need to be made about this. The first is that storytelling represents a *functional* Calvinism. I have emphasized the word *functional* here, because clearly there are authors, many good ones, who are not Calvinists and who might be disposed to argue this point with me. Fine, but let me make it first.

Every author stands in a *comparable* relation to the world he has created as God stands with the world *he* has created. It is comparable because, as you recall, we are imitating God. A potter is imitating God when he shapes the clay. A playwright is imitating God when he inscribes life into his characters. This is why this human relation can serve as an illustration of the divine relation. Take this illustration from Lewis, for example: "God can no more be in competition with a creature than Shakespeare can be in competition with Viola."[21]

When we are talking about a character's motivations, there are two ways we can address the question. One is internal to the structure of the play, and the other has to do with the will of the author. It makes no sense to assign 70 percent of the play to the writer and 30 percent to the characters. The apportionment has to be 100 percent and 100 percent. And the more Shakespeare writes, the freer Viola gets. And that is what God does for us. Even Screwtape sees it—God wants beings "united to him but still distinct."[22]

Our natural and carnal reaction is to kick against this, arguing that *they* are fictional characters without eternal souls, whereas *we* have hopes, dreams, and aspirations. We call this a poor analogy for we are much more important than the fictional characters in a play. First, this objection stands equally well (or not) against Jeremiah's comparison of the potter and clay (Jer. 18:6). If this is a bad illustration, then so is that. Second, Lewis uses precisely this illustration. And, third, and far more important, such objections reveal why our defensiveness really arises. Nobody ever says that "this is a *terrible* way to illustrate divine sovereignty. God is *much* greater than Shakespeare." But, in fact, the distance between Shakespeare and God is light-years greater than the distance between Dogberry and Douglas. There is a school of thought that maintains that the distance between Dogberry and Douglas is just a couple of yards.

So we are greater than pots? Fine. God is much greater than any potter.

But this leads to the next point. An author is sovereign over his story, but a good author respects the ingredients and antecedents. A good author has affection and respect for his characters, and the better the author, the greater the respect. Run this out—the almighty

---

[21] Lewis, *The Problem of Pain*, 49.
[22] Lewis, *Screwtape Letters*, 38.

Author is not one who writes a novel with the flattest characters ever. No, it goes the other way. We do not have a choice just between the will of the author and the will of the character. We also must take into account the nature of the story.

And so this brings us to one last thing, a place where we modern Reformed can learn from Lewis.

Calvinism under Jove

Reformation Calvinism was born under Jove. It flourishes under Jove, and is spiritually healthy there. But for the last several centuries (at least), it has come under the baneful influence of Saturn. Am I revealing here that Lewis has gotten way too much of his discarded image into my head? Will I be having dryads leading our small-group Bible studies next?

Now for those who dismiss my "pagan tomfoolery"—planetary influences and theology *indeed*—with a sneer and say that *they* want a Calvinism under *Christ*, thank you, Calvinism without centaurs, the better to enable us to get back to our gospel-preserving debates about supralapsarianism, not to mention how many eggs your wife is allowed to cook on the Lord's Day, several things have to be said.

First, I would suggest (mildly) you haven't understood the point. Nobody around here has any sympathy for pagan unbelief and superstition. Christ is Lord, and only Christ. But when the point is misunderstood this way, folks haven't understood it because they are under the baneful influences of Saturn. Jove and Saturn are metaphors, but they are not *just* metaphors. The fact that you can wring out the Westminster Confession of Faith like it was a damp washcloth does not mean that you don't have a case of the saturnine jimjams. Speaking of metaphor, I fear I might be overdoing it. But I am almost done.

Second, this is not a minor issue. Just as Lucy and Susan wouldn't feel safe around Bacchus unless Aslan was around, neither do I. But I also don't feel safe around Calvinists under Saturn. Calvinism without Jesus is deadly. When these precious doctrines of ours are used to perpetuate gloom, severity, introspection, accusations, morbidity, slander, gnat-strangling, and more, the soul is not safe.

Third, the original Protestants, and the Puritans *especially*, were not at all under Saturn. Here is Lewis describing the Puritans, and it is worthwhile reflecting on why there are so many surprises in these few sentences:

> But there is no understanding the period of the Reformation in England until we have grasped the fact that the quarrel between the Puritans and the Papists was not primarily a quarrel between rigorism and indulgence, and that, in so far as it was, the rigorism was on the Roman side. On many questions, and specially in their view of the marriage bed, the Puritans were the indulgent party; if we may without disrespect so use the name of a great Roman Catholic, a great writer, and a great man, they were much more Chestertonian than their adversaries.[23]

Where did *that* come from? It came from Lewis's thorough acquaintance with the primary sources left to us by *our* fathers, and that legacy is a large contributor to my willingness to luxuriate in my quite oxymoronic goal of becoming and remaining a Chestertonian Calvinist.

And, fourth, with this as the good news, over the last generation there have been a number of indications that our self-imposed, saturnine exile may be coming to an end. Many Calvinists are again becoming jovial—which should not be reduced to a willingness to tell the occasional joke. The issue is much deeper than that—we are talking about rich worship, robust psalm-singing laden with harmonies, laughter and Sabbath-feasting, exuberant preaching, and all with gladness and simplicity of heart. The winter is breaking. This is not just a thaw but promises to be a real spring.

---

[23] C. S. Lewis, "Donne and Love Poetry" (1938), in *Selected Literary Essays* (Cambridge, UK: Cambridge University Press, 1979), 116.

4

IN BRIGHT SHADOW

C. S. Lewis on the Imagination for Theology and Discipleship

KEVIN VANHOOZER

There are worse insults than being called a "sleeper." Yes, sloth is one of the seven deadly sins, but when I saw sloth portrayed on stage in a performance of Christopher Marlowe's play *Dr. Faustus*, it was hard to see what was so deadly about it. The other sins—pride, greed, lust—looked ugly, but sloth, a young girl, came onto the stage, stretched, yawned, and lay down. The audience relaxed with her. What harm is there in a catnap? None at all. Why, then, has the church classified sloth as a deadly sin? We don't hold someone blameworthy for being anemic or for not taking his five-hour energy drink every five hours. To be sure, drowsiness is culpable in certain situations: none of us wants our pilots falling asleep at the controls. Yet sloth is not mere sleepiness or laziness but rather what Dorothy Sayers rightly identifies as the spiritual condition of despair: "It is the sin that believes in nothing, enjoys nothing, hates nothing, finds purpose in nothing, lives for nothing, and remains alive because there is nothing for which it will die."[1]

---

[1] Dorothy L. Sayers, *Christian Letters to a Post-Christian World: A Selection of Essays* (Grand Rapids, MI: Eerdmans, 1969), 152.

Sleeper, Awake!

If the besetting sin of modernity is pride (an inordinate confidence in know-it-all reason), then that of postmodernity is sloth, a despairing indifference to truth. Someone who believes in nothing and lives for nothing might as well be asleep. Sloth is the ultimate sin of omission: sloth sits still, unmoved by anything real. Sleeping through a movie may not be deadly, but sitting on your hands while the cinema is burning around you certainly is. We must guard against sloth, the temptation to be lulled to sleep when there is something urgent to be done. Is there a cure for this spiritual narcolepsy? There is. Says G. K. Chesterton of Thomas Aquinas, the great medieval theologian, that when he was troubled by doubt, he chose to believe in *more* reality, not less. Aquinas has a kindred spirit in C. S. Lewis.

Lewis experienced a powerful awakening and afterwards did everything he could to stay awake, by which I mean spiritually alert to the opportunities, and dangers, that attend the Christian life. For Lewis, waking is a way of describing one's conversion, a coming to new life. The Christian life is all about wakefulness. Theology describes what we see when we are awake, in faith to the reality of God, and discipleship is the project of becoming *fully* awake to this reality and *staying* awake.

The sad truth is that many of us are, at best, only half awake. We think we're engaged with the real world—you know, the world of stock markets, stock-car racing, and stockpiles of chemical weapons—but in fact we're living in what Lewis calls the "shadowlands." We think we're awake, but we're really only daydreaming. We're sleepwalking our way through life—asleep at the wheel of existence—only semi-conscious of the eternal, those things that are truly solid that bear the weight of glory.

We want to believe the Bible—we do believe it, we confess the truth of its teaching, and we're prepared to defend it—but we nevertheless find ourselves unable to see our world in biblical terms, and that produces a feeling of disparity, an existential disconnect. If faith's influence is waning, as two-thirds of Americans apparently now think, then it is largely because of a failure of the evangelical imagination. We're suffering from imaginative malnutrition.

We typically associate sleep with dreaming, the imagination with daydreaming. But what if what we normally consider wakefulness is actually a kind of sleep? Read from this letter, written by Lewis in 1963, to one of his correspondents, a hospital patient at the time, weighed down with worries of her mortality. Lewis writes,

> Think of yourself just as a seed patiently waiting in the earth: waiting to come up a flower in the Gardener's good time, up into the *real* world, the real waking. I suppose that our whole present life, looked back on from there, will seem only a drowsy half-waking. We are here in the land of dreams. But the cock-crow is coming.[2]

If conversion is the moment of awakening to the reality of God, discipleship is the effort we make to stay awake.[3] Waking and sleeping often figure in Lewis's stories at important moments. Consider the scene in *The Silver Chair* when the Queen of Underland is holding Jill, Eustace, and Puddleglum captive in her subterranean lair. The Queen tries to convince them that there is no world outside her cavern. She creates an atmosphere thick with a drowsy smell, soft music—and then, like the Serpent in the garden, she lies through her teeth, "There is no land called Narnia." Puddleglum protests that he has come from "up there," and the witch makes the idea seem ridiculous: "Is there a country up among the stones and mortars of the roof?" Jill begins to succumb to the spell, saying, "No, I suppose that other world must be all a dream." "Yes," says the witch, "There never was any world but mine."[4]

---

[2] C. S. Lewis, letter to Mary Willis Shelburne, June 28, 1963, in *The Collected Letters of C. S. Lewis, vol. 3: Narnia, Cambridge, and Joy, 1950–1963*, ed. Walter Hooper (San Francisco: HarperSanFrancisco, 2007), 1,434 (emphasis original).

[3] "The real labour is to remember, to attend [to the presence of God]. In fact, to come awake. Still more, to remain awake." C. S. Lewis, *Letters to Malcolm* (London: Geoffrey Bles, 1964), 75.

[4] C. S. Lewis, *The Silver Chair* (New York: HarperCollins, 1981), chap. 12.

With the last of her waking strength, Jill suddenly remembers Aslan, but the witch responds that a lion is only a big cat: "And look how you can put nothing into your make-believe without copying it from the real world, this world of mine, which is the only world." Just before they all nod off for good, Puddleglum does something that makes Marsh-wiggles everywhere proud: he stamps his foot in the fire. This clears his head sufficiently for him to give the following speech: "Suppose we *have* only dreamed, or made up, all those things—trees and grass and sun . . . and Aslan. Suppose we have. Then all I can say is that, in that case, the made-up things seem a good deal more important than the real ones. . . . I'm going to live as like a Narnian as I can even if there isn't any Narnia."[5]

Those who follow Jesus Christ have been similarly jolted awake, not by stamping feet in the fire but by having descend on them tongues of fire. Remember the words of John the Baptist: "I baptize you with water. . . . He will baptize you with the Holy Spirit and fire" (Matt. 3:11). The Spirit of Christ burns in our hearts, awakening us to the presence and activity of Jesus Christ. Sleeper, awake! The full quotation comes from the apostle Paul, in Ephesians 5:14: "Awake, O sleeper, and arise from the dead, and Christ will shine on you." Lewis wants us to wake up, to live not in the shadowlands but in broad daylight—and he thinks the imagination can help. This, then, is our challenge: to understand *how Lewis enlists the imagination in the cause of wakefulness rather than daydreaming*.

Christianity has nothing to do with make-believe or wish fulfillment. There's nothing romantic about crucifixion, nothing more nitty-gritty than nails piercing flesh, and nothing airy-fairy about bodily resurrection. I'm a theologian, and I'm the least superstitious person you'll ever meet. I'm a realist who believes the world to be independent of what I say or think about it—but I'm also convinced that preachers and theologians minister reality. The question is: what's the nature of reality? How can we come to know the truth about *what is*?

---

[5] Ibid., 190–91 (emphasis original).

what is real?

Lewis had a high regard for Plato, perhaps because he too understood men and women to be dwellers in the shadowlands. Plato's famous Myth of the Cave suggests that we are all cave men and cave women, prisoners in a dark place, chained so that we face a wall on which are cast the shadows of the things that pass by the cave's mouth. It's worse than the witch's underworld, because cave dwellers who have never been outside have no way of knowing the reality behind the shadow appearances. In Plato's view, the world that appears to our senses is only a shadow world: we need Reason to see, with our mind's eye, the eternal Forms of which things on earth are pale images. For Plato, reason, not imagination, is the royal road out of the shadowlands into the bright land of reality.

Karl Marx didn't say, "Sleepers, awake," but "Workers, unite!" But he too believed that he could lead people out of their industrial caves into the light of communism. Marx wants us to wake up not to Plato's ethereal realm of "Ideas" but to the material and economic forces that, he thinks, shape our lives and determine history "from below." Marx was suspicious of religion and imagination alike: combined, they comprise the "opiate of the people" because they distract us, with pious fiction, from what is truly real, namely, the class warfare that makes the world go round.

I hope you agree that it is vitally important to awaken to the truth of what is happening in our world. But what is the reality behind the veil of appearances? Is truth "above," as Plato thinks, or "below," as Marx claims? And is the imagination a hindrance or help in waking up to the truth?

In responding to this question, we do well to begin by considering Lewis's own awakening: his conversion to Christianity. Then we'll want to hear what Lewis has to say about the imagination, discipleship, and theology. After that, we'll run a second lap, circling round the same three themes once more, this time from the perspective of how I employ them in my own work as a theologian. We'll conclude with some thoughts about how the imagination helps us answer two questions: who is Jesus Christ for us today, and who are we for him?

Lewis's Own Awakening: *Phantastes*

"Awake, O sleeper, and arise from the dead, and Christ will shine on you" (Eph. 5:14). This is the apostle Paul's rousing conclusion to his exhortation to the church at Ephesus to walk not in darkness but "as children of light" (Eph. 5:8). Note the relation between waking and walking. Conversion is like waking, and walking is like discipleship, and we need the light of Christ for both. We are awake and alive in Christ, the light of the world. Here in Ephesians 5:8–14, Paul describes the process by which those who were once in darkness come to walk in the light.[6] He's thinking about conversion, and some commentators think this passage was associated with early Christian baptism.

Lewis's own awakening, or at least the first stage of his awakening, began with what he describes as the "baptism of his imagination."[7] As a child, he had had moments of joy, intense intimations of something wonderful just beyond his reach, a wood beyond the world's end, but he had become, under the tutelage of his rationalist teachers, an adolescent atheist, a teenage Richard Dawkins. In a letter to his friend Arthur Greeves, Lewis declared, "I believe in no religion." Religions are mythologies invented to meet our emotional needs.[8] In *Surprised by Joy*, however, he explains what happened to him after purchasing George MacDonald's *Phantastes* at a railway station. When he stepped onto the train, he was a split personality: "Nearly all I loved I believed to be imaginary; nearly all that I believed to be real I thought grim and meaningless."[9] But as he read MacDonald's book later that evening, he began to experience a radical makeover.

The light of Christ shone on Lewis as he read *Phantastes*. He did

---

[6] Peter T. O'Brien, *The Letter to the Ephesians*. Pillar New Testament Commentary (Grand Rapids, MI: Eerdmans, 1999), 372.

[7] C. S. Lewis, ed., *George MacDonald: An Anthology* (New York: Macmillan, 1947), xxxii–xxxiii.

[8] C. S. Lewis, letter to Arthur Greeves, October 1916, in *The Collected Letters of C. S. Lewis, vol. 1: Family Letters 1905–1931*, ed. Walter Hooper (San Francisco: HarperSanFrancisco, 2004), 230–31.

[9] C. S. Lewis, *Surprised by Joy: The Shape of My Early Life* (London: Geoffrey Bles, 1955), 170.

not yet confess the light as Christ, but whose other embassy could it be? Lewis says he experienced what as a boy he called "Northerness": a bright shadow, a glimpse of the beauty of another world that awakened a yearning both for that world and for the experience of desiring that world. Here is how he describes reading *Phantastes*: "But now I saw the bright shadow coming out of the book into the real world and resting there, transforming all common things and yet itself unchanged. Or, more accurately, I saw the common things drawn into the bright shadow."[10] This bright shadow was not quite "Northerness," but otherness—yet instead of remaining other, this other world leapt out of the story, landing on the Normandy Beach of Lewis's imagination and invading his sixteen-year-old secular consciousness.

Phantastes did not convert his intellect; other books did that. But it did insert a new quality into his waking life: holiness. That's the quality Lewis later said he found in *Phantastes*—a holy Northerness that was also a wholly otherness—a quality that refused to remain in the world of the text and instead began to cast a bright shadow over the world in which Lewis lived: "I saw the common things drawn into the bright shadow."[11] I want us to understand this dynamic.

For the moment, let's just say that young Mr. Lewis experienced a spiritual awakening. MacDonald helped him to see a bright silver lining to earthly clouds, a deeper dimension to ordinary earthly things, a world beyond cold logic and physical matter. The bright shadow in *Phantastes* that so intrigued Lewis turns out "to be [a supernatural] quality of the real universe . . . in which we all live."[12] Thirty years after picking up *Phantastes*, Lewis wrote, "I have never concealed the fact that I regard [MacDonald] as my master; indeed, I fancy I have never written a book in which I did not quote from him."[13] MacDonald even appears as a character in *The Great Divorce*. You remember

---

[10] Ibid., 181.
[11] Ibid.
[12] Lewis, *MacDonald*, xxxiv.
[13] Ibid., xxxii.

the story: it's about not the hound of heaven but a Greyhound to heaven, a bus trip from the "Valley of the Shadow of Life" to the outskirts of heaven. That's where Lewis meets MacDonald, whom he casts in the role of his guide to heaven, the Virgil to his Dante, and tries to tell him how formative reading *Phantastes* had been. It was, says Lewis, "what the first sight of Beatrice had been to Dante: *Here begins the New Life.*"[14]

Lewis does well to associate waking and walking in considering new life in Christ. The Christian life is all about waking up and walking out of the shadowlands toward the sun. Lewis's mention of Mac-Donald as his Virgil recalls Dante's *Divine Comedy*, where Virgil—a poet, not a philosopher—leads Dante further up and further in. We Protestants have our own version: John Bunyan's *Pilgrim's Progress*. The Christian life is indeed a life of itinerant discipleship, and Lewis's journey began with the baptism of his imagination.

Lewis on the Imagination: From Baptism to Discipleship

We turn now to the imagination's role not in bringing us to but rather in helping us to abide in Christ. Lewis has taught me that the triune God not only baptizes but also *disciples* our imaginations. He has also persuaded me that the imagination is a vital ingredient in doing theology. Not everyone is convinced. When in doubt, define your terms.

Discipleship

We start with discipleship. Walter Hooper says that Lewis was the most thoroughly converted person he ever met. Lewis desired above all to submit not only his thought but also his whole life to Christ. Some of us may not have sufficiently appreciated the extent to which Lewis was a Christ-intoxicated man. It's therefore significant that the opening line of the first volume of Paul Brazier's new trilogy on Lewis is: "This is a book about Jesus Christ."[15]

---

[14] C. S. Lewis, *The Great Divorce* (New York: HarperCollins, 2001), 66 (emphasis original).

[15] Paul Brazier, *C. S. Lewis: Revelation, Conversion, and Apologetics* (Eugene, OR: Pickwick, 2012), 1.

Christian discipleship is for Lewis the process of becoming Christ-like. God is not interested in making merely nice people (this is the lie of moral therapeutic deism); he wants to make people perfect, like Christ. Paul says in Romans 8:29 that God predestines those whom he foreknew "to be conformed to the image of his Son." What interests Lewis is how God translates Christ into ordinary mortals.

We may not want to become little Christs, but the Lord will not settle for anything less. Lewis imagines Christ telling would-be disciples to count the cost of following him: "'Make no mistake,' He says, 'if you let me, I will make you perfect. The moment you put yourself in My hands, that is what you are in for."[16] Indeed, the church "exists for nothing else but to draw men into Christ, to make them little Christs. If they are not doing that, all the cathedrals, clergy, missions, sermons, even the Bible itself, are simply a waste of time"[17]—and we can certainly add theology to that list.

Theology

And speaking of theology, what exactly did Lewis think it was good for? When Sheldon Vanauken wrote asking whether he should switch from studying English to theology, Lewis replied with some ambivalence: "I've always been glad myself that Theology is not the thing I earn my living by. . . . The performance of a *duty* will probably teach you quite as much about God as academic Theology would do."[18] Ouch.

In fact, Lewis was an amateur theologian in the best sense of the term: one who does something not to earn one's living but simply for the love of it—for the love of God. Lewis wrote introductions to theological tomes such as Athanasius's *On the Incarnation*, depicted doctrines such as the fall and the atonement in his fiction, and explained nothing less than the doctrine of the Trinity in the radio broadcasts eventually published as *Mere Christianity*. Think about that—talking

---

[16] C. S. Lewis, *Mere Christianity* (Glasgow: Collins, 1955), 158.
[17] Ibid., 171.
[18] Lewis, *Collected Letters, vol. 3*, 83 (emphasis original).

about the doctrine of the Trinity on the radio. That's the equivalent of an amateur trapeze artist doing triple somersaults without a net.

Here's how Lewis begins: "Everyone has warned me not to tell you what I am going to tell you. . . . They all say 'the ordinary reader does not want Theology; give him plain practical religion.' I have rejected their advice. I do not think the ordinary reader is such a fool."[19] Lewis goes on to compare doctrines to maps. Maps help orient us, help us find our way in the real world. The doctrine of the Trinity maps out as it were the life of God, and the Trinitarian missions—the Father sending the Son; Father and Son sending the Spirit—enable us to share in the Son's fellowship with the Father. To share in the Son's life is to have a share in something that was begotten, not made, something that has always existed and always will exist.[20] Lewis concludes: "I warned you that theology is practical. The whole purpose for which we exist is to be . . . taken into the life of God."[21]

What difference does theology make? Just this: it wakes us up to the reality of our sonship, our adoption into God's family, our being in Christ. Theology uses both prayer and poetry to minister this reality. Prayer is a way of directing the mind to what is ultimately real: our createdness and God's creativity. "Now the moment of prayer," says Lewis, "is for me . . . the awareness, the re-awakened awareness that this 'real world' and 'real self' are very far from being rock-bottom realities."[22] Prayer is the preeminent theological act, and disciples do theology when they experience the reality of their relationship to God on their knees.

A disciple is one who prays—and stays awake. This is easier said than done. While Jesus prayed at the garden of Gethsemane, reminding himself of what was real and steeling himself to face death, his disciples fell asleep. Jesus found them, reprimanded Peter, and encouraged him to "keep awake and pray" (Mark 14:38 NRSV). They

[19] Lewis, *Mere Christianity*, 131.
[20] Ibid., 150.
[21] Ibid., 138.
[22] Lewis, *Letters to Malcolm*, 81.

fell asleep again, and when Jesus returned, Mark tells us, "they did not know what to say to him" (Mark 14:40 NRSV). Jesus went away once more and, you guessed it, the disciples fell asleep again. By failing to stay awake, they effectively denied him three times. *They* literally fell asleep; my concern is that disciples today are metaphorically drifting off, sleepwalking their way through life and thus missing the bright shadows of eternity in the everyday. The imagination can help.

The Socratic Club of Oxford University once asked Lewis to address the question, "Is Theology Poetry?" which he took to be asking, Does theology owe its attraction to the power of arousing and satisfying our imagination and, if so, are we mistaking aesthetic enjoyment for intellectual assent?[23] If theology is poetry, Lewis observes, it is not very good poetry. There is nothing particularly aesthetic about the drunkenness of Noah or the thorn in Paul's flesh.

On the other hand, theology uses figurative language, and Lewis says we cannot restate our belief in a form free from metaphor: "We can say, if you like, 'God entered history' instead of saying 'God came down to earth.' But, of course, 'entered' is just as metaphorical as 'came down.' . . . All language about things other than physical objects is necessarily metaphorical."[24] What is metaphor if not a statement that, taken literally, proves false? What are we to make of Lewis's suggestion, in a chapter called "Let's Pretend" (in *Mere Christianity*), that when we pray "Our Father," we are "dressing up as Christ"?[25] The answer lies in Lewis's understanding of the imagination, which involves a "good pretending"—a way of waking up and remaining wakeful and attentive to reality.

Imagination

Wait a moment: how can imagining that we are something we're not (which is what pretending is) ever help us to come to grips with reality? Should it not worry us that the King James Version consistently

[23] C. S. Lewis, "Is Theology Poetry?," in *Screwtape Proposes a Toast* (London: Fontana, 1965), 42.
[24] Lewis, "Is Theology Poetry?," 53–54.
[25] Lewis, *Mere Christianity*, 158.

refers to *vain* imaginings (e.g., Ps. 2:1; Rom. 1:21), or that Genesis 6:5 says, "God saw that the wickedness of man was great in the earth, and that every imagination of the thoughts of his heart was only evil continually"? Ironically enough, a *picture* of the imagination—as a faculty for producing mental images, often of things that are not there—holds many Christians captive. Representing things that are absent or nonexistent sounds suspiciously like lying: saying of what is *not* that it is. On the standard picture, the imagination produces false images more conducive to idolatry than theology. Is this what Lewis has in mind: the imagination as a picture-making power? Before I answer that, let's consider what Lewis's master, George Mac-Donald, thought about imagination.

MacDonald did one thing Lewis never did: he came to the States and went on a lecture tour. It was a huge success; there had been nothing like it since Charles Dickens's visit. In gratitude for his warm welcome, MacDonald wrote and published "Letter to American Boys" in 1878. It's a long letter and includes a story that begins like this: "There was once a wise man to whom was granted the power to send forth his thoughts in shapes that other people could see."[26] The "power" to which MacDonald refers is the imagination. Elsewhere MacDonald gives a formal definition: the imagination is "that faculty which gives form to thought."[27] When forms are new embodiments of old truths, we say they are products of the Imagination, but if they are mere inventions, however lovely, they are works of Fancy. According to MacDonald, creation itself is the work of the divine imagination. The world is made up of God's thoughts put into shapes that people can see.[28]

What about Lewis? Did he ever define the imagination? Like fortification, the process of making forts, or clarification, the process of

---

[26] Cited in George MacDonald, *The Gifts of the Child Christ: Fairytales and Stories for the Childlike*, vol. 1 (Grand Rapids, MI: Eerdmans, 1973), 11.
[27] George MacDonald, "The Imagination: Its Function and Its Culture," in *A Dish of Orts: Chiefly Papers on the Imagination, and on Shakspere* (London: Sampson Low, Marston, 1895), 2.
[28] See Kerry Dearborn, *Baptized Imagination: The Theology of George MacDonald* (Surrey, UK: Ashgate, 2006).

making clear, *imagination* suggests the process or faculty of making images. Lewis acknowledges this common use of the term to designate the mental faculty by which we make images or pictures of things, but he uses the term in other ways as well. Owen Barfield suggests that the reason Lewis never developed an overarching theory of imagination was that he wanted to protect it, not subject it to analysis. Analysis is the work of reason, but Lewis is convinced that the imagination has a cognitive vocation of its own.

Reason is the faculty of analysis that seeks objectivity, inspects things, and then breaks them down into their component parts. In his essay "Meditation in a Toolshed," Lewis contrasts looking *at* a beam of light with looking *along* it. Reason remains aloof, maintaining a critical distance from the shaft of light, observing only the swirling particles of dust. Imagination, by way of contrast, steps into the beam of light and looks along it, tasting and participating in its illumination. Is it possible that Lewis intends his "Meditation in a Toolshed" to correct Plato's "Myth of the Cave," with its high view of speculative Reason? It's possible. For Plato, the world is full of shadows (appearances) and only Reason apprehends the Eternal Forms (truth). For Lewis, the world is full of bright shadows, but it is the imagination that perceives the brightness—the holy otherness—in the shadow. Things on earth are the created form of divine thoughts. Or as Lewis puts it in a letter to his friend Arthur Greeves: "Christianity is God expressing Himself through what we call 'real things.'"[29]

Fallen human beings both express and ensnare themselves by making false mental images; our mind's eye suffers the distortion of the astigmatism of sin.[30] But we should no more hold the imagination itself responsible for making false images than we hold Reason responsible for logical fallacies. Fancies and fallacies alike proceed from bent hearts, not from the divinely created faculties of Imagination and Reason.

---

[29] C. S. Lewis, letter to Arthur Greeves, in *They Stand Together: The Letters of C. S. Lewis to Arthur Greeves (1914–1963)*, ed. Walter Hooper (New York: Macmillan, 1979), 428.
[30] See his Dec. 14, 1955, letter to Dorothy Sayers, in *Collected Letters, vol. 3*, 683–84.

Entire books have been written on the relation of reason and imagination in Lewis. We have time to ponder only one comment: "For me, reason is the natural organ of truth; but imagination is the organ of meaning. Imagination, producing new metaphors or revivifying old, is not the cause of truth, but its condition."[31] This is a hard saying. What is an organ of meaning? I believe it has something to do with the capacity not only to liken one thing to another but also to discover patterns, to synthesize things that initially appear unrelated. Where Reason excels in taking things apart and analyzing individual puzzle pieces, the imagination perceives the whole of which the pieces are a part. Imagination is the organ of discerning meaningful patterns. It is the power of insight, that Eureka moment when all the parts fall into place, transforming what would otherwise be an incoherent jumble into a meaningful whole.

Metaphor reminds us that imagination works with verbal as well as visual raw material. Metaphors describe the unfamiliar in terms of the more familiar. "Chess is war" makes us think about the game of chess in terms drawn from military experience. This association of ideas generates meaning—and power. George Lakoff and Mark Johnson talk about metaphors we live by.[32] "Time is money." Such metaphors color our daily experience. If we walk around thinking "life is war," that will structure what we do and how we do it differently than if our leading thought was Forrest Gump's "Life is a box of chocolates" or, for that matter, John Calvin's "Life is a theater in which to act for God's glory."

One factor that kept the young Lewis from embracing Christianity was his inability to understand what it meant to "be saved." In particular, he could not understand the atonement, at least not when it was formulated as an abstract doctrinal truth. He didn't know what the doctrine *meant*. He wrote to Arthur Greeves: "You can't believe a

---

[31] C. S. Lewis, "Bluspels and Flalansferes: A Semantic Nightmare," in *Selected Literary Essays*, ed. Walter Hooper (Cambridge, UK: Cambridge University Press, 1969), 251–65.
[32] George Lakoff and Mark Johnson, *Metaphors We Live By* (Chicago: University of Chicago Press, 1980).

thing when you are ignorant *what* the thing is."[33] Here is where the imagination, the organ of meaning, comes into its own. The New Testament uses several metaphors to communicate the saving significance of Jesus's death: sacrifice, penalty, ransom, victory, and so forth. Lewis came to understand the doctrine of atonement only when he contemplated it through those metaphors.

Metaphors minister understanding by forming meaningful associations. Metaphors are the building blocks for the house in which we live, the interpretive framework we inhabit. But the house itself is not metaphor; this honor goes to story and myth. A story "is only imagining out loud."[34] Stories, too, are organs of meaning insofar as they connect the scattered parts of a person's life and transform them into a unity with a beginning, middle, and end. Myths are stories, too, though what counts is the pattern of events rather than the telling. Myths do not simply communicate ideas but allow us to see and taste the reality of what they are about. The very best stories communicate the "feel" of reality, awaking something deep within us. In Lewis's words: "What flows into you from the myth is not truth but reality (truth is always *about* something, but reality is that *about which* truth is)."[35] We taste the truth when we indwell the story or when the story indwells us.

Lewis wrote stories not so readers could escape but so that they could *experience* reality, and not its surface either but rather its supernatural *depths*. Lewis did not put reason on the side of truth and imagination on the side of falsehood. No, both reason and imagination can communicate truth, but reason does it in bits and pieces while the imagination grasps the big picture, how things fit together, and allows us to feel as true what reason treats only as abstractions.[36] Stories wake us up to the meaningful patterns of life. The imagina-

---

[33] Lewis, letter to Arthur Greeves, in *They Stand Together*, 427 (emphasis original).

[34] C. S. Lewis, letter to Mrs. Johnson, March 2, 1955, in *Collected Letters, vol. 3*, 575.

[35] C. S. Lewis, "Myth Became Fact," in *God in the Dock: Essays on Theology and Ethics* (Grand Rapids, MI: Eerdmans, 1970), 66 (emphases original).

[36] See David Hein and Edward Henderson, eds., *C. S. Lewis and Friends: Faith and the Power of the Imagination* (Eugene, OR: Cascade, 2011), 4–5.

tion helps us to taste and see the goodness of God: the brightness in the shadowlands.

In his sermon "The Weight of Glory," Lewis speaks movingly about the desire we all have for something that eludes us. Our experiences of beauty are only the echo of a tune we have not heard, "news from a country we have never yet visited." Lewis then addresses the congregation: "Do you think I am trying to weave a spell? Perhaps I am; but remember your fairy tales. Spells are used for breaking enchantments as well as for inducing them. And you and I have need of the strongest spell that can be found to wake us from the evil enchantment of worldliness."[37] Lewis's imagination is not the opiate of the people but a dose of caffeine that snaps us awake. So are the stories of the Bible. For Lewis they refer "not to the nonhistorical but rather to the nondescribable."[38] And, as with metaphor, so with story: we can't say exactly what it is about apart from the story itself. In Lewis's words: "The 'doctrines' we get *out of* the true myth are of course *less* true: they are translations into our *concepts* and *ideas* of that which God has already expressed in a language more adequate, namely the actual incarnation, crucifixion, and resurrection."[39] Scripture is the story that disciples live by. Scripture tells us the true story of the wood beyond the world where mankind fell, the true story of the Word made flesh, who became one of us so that we could become one of him. Disciples need imagination to indwell the story of the Christ—to see, taste, and feel the risen one in our midst.

In Bright Shadow: Faith Seeking Understanding and *What Is* "in Christ"

Let me now restate in my own terms what I have learned from Lewis.

---

[37] C. S. Lewis, "The Weight of Glory," in *Screwtape Proposes a Toast*, 98.
[38] Corbin Scott Carnell, *Bright Shadow of Reality: Spiritual Longing in C. S. Lewis* (Grand Rapids, MI: Eerdmans, 1974), 106.
[39] Lewis, letter to Arthur Greeves, in *They Stand Together*, 428 (emphases original).

Theology, Discipleship, and the Parabolic Imagination

Theology ministers understanding, enabling disciples to act out their knowledge of God. Theology is eminently practical. It is all about waking up to the real, to *what is*—specifically, to *what is* "in Christ." It takes imagination to see *what is in Christ*, for Christ is the meaning of the whole, the ultimate pattern in whom all things are held together (Col. 1:17).

Disciples demonstrate understanding by conforming to what is in Christ. To be a disciple is to know Jesus Christ and to put that knowledge into practice. There are no armchair disciples; there is no alibi for discipleship. One can't be a disciple *in theory*. No, *doctrines are what disciples live by*, because doctrines inform us what is in Christ. Creation, incarnation, Trinity, and atonement are not abstractions to be thought but meaningful patterns to be lived.[40] *The imagination helps disciples act out what is in Christ*. Theology exchanges the false pictures that hold us captive with biblical truth, disciplining our imaginations with sound doctrine. Discipleship is a matter of this "indoctrinated" imagination.

Disciples must beware of having their imaginations taken captive or being put to sleep. Many of Screwtape's strategies have to do with capturing the disciple's imagination. If you can control the metaphors and stories people live by, you've got them. I want to say, from my perch on George MacDonald's shoulders, that imagination is the faculty by which God gives created forms to his thoughts and *literary forms* to his words. Jesus used what we can call the parabolic imagination in giving story form to his thoughts about the kingdom of God. Similarly, disciples need the parabolic imagination in order to inhabit the kingdom of God on earth as it is in heaven.

Parables are extended metaphors. Jesus does not describe what the kingdom looks like; instead, he tells us what kinds of things happen there. The metaphors disciples live by are those that awaken them to the kingdom things God is doing in Christ. I'm haunted by

---

[40] Hein and Henderson, *C. S. Lewis and Friends*, 8.

what the sociologist Robert Bellah says: "The quality of a culture may be changed when two percent of its people have a new vision." Surely we can muster 2 percent! Unfortunately, if other sociologists are to be believed, an even greater percentage of Christians live by a quite different metaphor, namely, the moral metaphor of God as Father Christmas. Moral therapeutic deism indoctrinates its adherents to think of God not as worrying about their sanctification but rather whether they've been naughty or nice. It's no good professing to be a Christ follower if your imagination is captive to the image of God as a moral therapist or a celestial handyman whom we call upon only when we have a problem that needs fixing. In stark contrast, Lewis likens God to a savage beast, an un-housebroken member of the great cat family, to be precise: "He is not a tame lion."

The Nature of the Biblical Imagination

Standing on Lewis's shoulders, I see the biblical imagination as the organ of theological meaning. The Bible gives us the metaphors and stories disciples live by. However, too many evangelical congregations are suffering from malnourished imaginations that have been taken captive to culturally conditioned pictures of the good life. It is difficult to connect the materialistic, market-driven pictures of the good life with the sound doctrine by which disciples are to live. We want to believe the Bible—we do believe it; we are prepared to defend doctrinal truth—but for the life of us, we find ourselves unable to relate the doctrine we profess to the lifestyle we practice. We feel a discrepancy, a fateful disconnect, between the world in which we live and the system of theology we believe. The imagination can help. I have said that theology is about the new reality in Christ and discipleship is about participating in that new reality. I now want to say that imagination is the faculty that wakes us up to that new reality and helps us to stay awake.

Let me make two points about the nature of imagination as an organ of theological meaning:

First, the imagination is not merely a factory for producing mental images—especially of things that are not there—but a cognitive faculty for creating meaning through making and then verbalizing conceptual associations (i.e., likening). The imagination is a synthetic, synoptic power, a kind of part/whole thinking that enables us to fit things together in meaningful forms, including biblical stories. Call it the "biblical imagination."

Second, the imagination engages the will and emotions as well as the mind. Paul perhaps has the imagination in mind when, in Ephesians 1:18, he speaks of "having the eyes of your hearts enlightened." The Spirit alone can open the eyes of our heart, but we then have to make the effort to keep them open by maintaining a vital relationship with the object of our heart's desire: the Lord Jesus Christ.

The Function of the Biblical Imagination

Turning from the nature of the imagination to its function, let me make two further points. I can do it in four words, with two pairs of ideas: *this-that* and *present-perfect*.

The basic gesture of the imagination is the metaphorical invitation to see *this* as *that* (e.g., "This is my body"). We need imagination to understand how marriage (*this*) symbolizes the relationship of Christ and his church (*that*).

Here we do well to recall the possibility of false imaginings, evil spells. Disciples must not confuse the evangelical *what is* and *what will be in Christ* with the satanic *what if* or *what might be* apart from Christ. The Serpent in the garden played on Eve's imagination, saying that if only she would eat of the tree in the middle of the garden, she would be "like God" (Gen. 3:5). Satan played the same *what if* game with Jesus, showing him all the kingdoms of the earth and saying, "If you, then, will worship me, it will all be yours" (Luke 4:7). In each case, the *what if* held out the possibility of a good coming from disobeying or violating the created order—in fact, no good at all.

Contrast the satanic *what if* with the Pauline *what is*. Theology's task is to say *what is in Christ*, and it needs the imagination to do so. Paul is not playing make-believe when he says he has been crucified with Christ. He does not say, "It is *as if* Christ lives in me." That would be a case of bad pretending and gets us no further than pious fiction. No, Paul says *what is* in Christ. It requires faith, and imagination, to see it, however, because being in Christ is not evident to the senses. Lewis had the unique gift of writing about *what if* in order to give us a taste of *what was, is, and will be* "in Christ."

And this brings me to the second function of the imagination: seeing not simply *this* as *that* but the *present-partial* as *future-perfect*. It takes imagination to understand Paul when he says, "I have been crucified with Christ. It is no longer I who live, but Christ who lives in me" (Gal. 2:20). Yes, Paul is a man "in Christ," but not as a shoe is in a shoebox. Paul *is* in Christ, but as President Clinton put it: it all depends on what the meaning of the word *is* is. The *is* of "what is in Christ" is *eschatological*: it has everything to do with *now* tasting the kingdom of God whose completion remains future. Thanks to the indwelling Holy Spirit, disciples *already* enjoy union with Christ, even though they have *not yet* attained to the full measure of Christlikeness. Doctrine that sets forth *what is in Christ* requires a robust eschatological imagining, a faith-based seeing that perceives what is *presently incomplete*—our salvation—as *already* finished. As Lewis reminds us, we've never talked to a "mere mortal": we are to take each other seriously because even the most uninteresting person "may one day be a creature which, if you saw it now, you would be strongly tempted to worship."[41]

What Lewis calls "good pretending" is not the fictive *what if* but the eschatological *what is*. Though the naked eye can't see it, the eyes of the heart see God's transferring saints from the old age to the new, from the kingdom of darkness to the kingdom of light (Col. 1:13). The eyes of the regenerate heart see those who put their trust in Jesus Christ as truly (i.e., eschatologically) united to him. To be

---

[41] Lewis, "The Weight of Glory," 109.

in Christ is to live and move and have our being in a new sphere, "transplanted into a new soil and a new climate, and both soil and climate are Christ."[42]

Putting It All Together: With Jesus on the Mountain

I can now state my thesis: *To imagine what is in Christ is not to daydream but to awake to the day of the Lord.* Calvin was right. The Scriptures are our spectacles of faith. We must look not simply *at* but *along* the Bible, especially if we want to see more than specks of doctrinal dust. The imagination is a way of looking along the Bible's metaphors, a way of indwelling its stories. When we look along and dwell in the text, we are imagining biblically: we are letting biblical patterns organize and interpret our experience. It is only by viewing the world through the stories of the Bible that we see God, the world, and ourselves as we truly are.

The biblically disciplined imagination sees reality as it truly is: not a mechanical universe in perpetual motion but rather a divine creation in the midst of labor pains, where the new in Christ struggles to come forth from the old in Adam. *Doctrine does not tell us to pretend to be something that we are not; it rather tells us who we really are: creatures in God's image with a mandate to image God.* Doctrine prepares disciples for their vocation, which is not play acting, but *being real*, that is, being participants in the kingdom of God that is really here in the midst of what is passing away, even if it is seen only through the eyes of a faithful heart. The task of discipleship is to act out the truth of Christian doctrine: in acting out what (eschatologically) is in Christ, we become *Christlike*.

Let me now pull together everything I've said by focusing on one crucial moment in the gospel story: Jesus's transfiguration. Once again three disciples accompany Jesus to pray, and once again they fall asleep. They were "heavy with sleep" (Luke 9:32). Meanwhile,

---

[42] James S. Stewart, *A Man in Christ: The Vital Elements of St. Paul's Religion* (Grand Rapids, MI: Baker, 1975), 157.

Jesus is transfigured: his clothes become dazzling white (a quality laundry-detergent makers promise but never deliver), and his face "shone like the sun" (Matt. 17:2). What's going on and what does it mean?

Here is what Luke says: "When they became fully awake they saw his glory and the two men who stood with him" (Luke 9:32). There are other accounts of people seeing bright lights and not knowing what to make of it (think of Paul's companions on the road to Damascus). Yet when the disciples awoke they saw something more than normal light; they saw Jesus's glory. What exactly did they see? What does *glory* look like? I believe they saw the eschatological *is*: Jesus had just predicted that some with him would not taste death before they saw the kingdom of God. This is precisely what Jesus's transfiguration showed them—a preview of his glorious lordship in the age to come. But the disciples needed a biblically informed imagination to see *this* as *that*. The evangelists go out of their way to make imaginative connections between Jesus's transfiguration and God's appearance to Israel on Mount Sinai in Exodus 24. Both incidents involve clouds, God's voice, and shining faces: Jesus's and Moses's. We catch the theological imagination at work in this connecting of the canonical dots.

Others had seen Jesus and watched him perform miracles yet did not know who he was; it takes a biblically disciplined imagination to see Jesus as the summation of the law and the prophets and to grasp how God is summing up all things in him (Eph. 1:10). The disciples who witnessed Jesus's transfiguration began to grasp the true significance of his person and work.

We are those disciples on the mountain with Jesus. Present-day Christians need to awaken to the glory of the transfigured, risen Christ in our midst, and we need to stay awake so that we, like the disciples, see "no one but Jesus only" (Matt. 17:8). "Veiled in flesh the Godhead see": disciples see the "fullness of God" (Col. 1:19) in Jesus not with physical eyes but with the eyes of the heart. Jesus is the bright shadow—not "Northerness" but Holy Otherness—in human form, coming out of the Good Book into the real world and resting there, transforming all common things. Here is the marvel: the one whose story the Bible tells is not confined to that story. He is Lord, and he is here. To see the common things of daily life drawn into the bright shadow of the Christ—this is the mark of a well-nourished theological imagination. It is precisely the biblically formed and transformed imagination that helps disciples wake up and stay awake to what is, and will be, in Christ Jesus.

An Edifying Conclusion

I cannot recall a time when I was not living in or acting out stories. Thanks to Alexander Dumas and Roger Lancelyn Green, what would have otherwise been a fairly plain tract of single-family homes was, for me, a kingdom wherein I could exercise chivalry, rescue fair ten-year-old maidens, and defend my honor against the dragon next door (an elderly mean lady, truth be told). It was the imagination that allowed me to inhabit the worlds of novels such as *The Three Musketeers* or *King Arthur and his Knights of the Round Table*. They were very much part of my early education. They gave me not so much abstract principles of behavior but concrete examples: here is how heroes behave when villains oppress the helpless. I knew, of course, that I could not really harm the neighborhood bully, much less run him through with a sword. Still, I look back fondly on the time spent between the covers—of books and bed sheets—as an important part of my character development. Years later I discovered C. S. Lewis, and I realized that behind the kingdom I had discovered in Dumas, there was *another* kingdom, deeper, more compelling, more exciting, and more real: the kingdom of God. I became a knight of the *Lord's* Table.

A final illustration. Two stonemasons were hard at work. When asked what they were doing, the first said: "I am cutting this stone in a perfectly square shape." The other answered: "I am building a cathedral."[43] Both answers are correct, but it takes imagination to see that you are building a cathedral, not simply making blocks of granite. Two pastors were hard at work. When asked what they were doing, the first said: "I am planning programs, preparing sermons, and managing conflict." The other answered: "I am building a temple." It takes the biblical imagination to see one's congregation as a living temple, with each member a living stone (1 Pet. 2:5) being worked—chiseled, fitted, and polished—in order to be joined together with Christ, the cornerstone (Eph. 2:20). It takes the eschatological imagination to look at a sinner and see a saint.

"Therefore stay awake—for you do not know when the master of the house will come, in the evening, or at midnight, or when the rooster crows, or in the morning" (Mark 13:35).

Disciples need imagination to stay awake to the reality of what is in Christ. To be in bright shadow is to live in the shadowlands *as* people with eyes of the heart enlightened, alert to the mystery of grace in the mundane, awake to God in the ordinary. Disciples may live in the shadowlands, but we "walk as children of light" (Eph. 5:8), "as he is in the light" (1 John 1:7). To live as a disciple is to live in the bright shadow of Jesus Christ.

"Awake, O sleeper, and arise from the dead, and Christ will shine on you" (Eph. 5:14).

---

[43] I am indebted for this illustration to Etienne Wenger, *Communities of Practice: Learning, Meaning, and Identity* (Cambridge, UK: Cambridge University Press, 1999), 176.

5

C. S. LEWIS ON HEAVEN AND THE NEW EARTH

God's Eternal Remedy to the Problem of Evil and Suffering

RANDY ALCORN

I grew up in a home without Christ. My dad was a tavern owner who despised Christians in general and pastors in particular. My parents had both been divorced, and their fights left me worried that another was on its way.

Though I seemed okay on the outside, inside I felt a gnawing emptiness. Comic books and science fiction were my escape. I yearned for something bigger than myself. I'd study the stars and planets and every clear night gaze at them for hours through my telescope. One night I discovered the great galaxy of Andromeda, with its trillion stars, 2.5 million light-years away. I was filled with awe. I longed to go there and explore its wonders and lose myself in something greater than myself.

My wonder was trumped by an unbearable sense of loneliness and separation. I wanted to worship, but I didn't know whom. I wept because I felt so incredibly small. Unknown to me, God was using the wonders of the universe to draw me to himself. As Romans 1 says, I was seeing in what he had made "his invisible attributes . . . his eternal power and divine nature" (v. 20).

One night several years later, I opened a Bible and saw these words for the first time: "In the beginning, God created the heavens and the earth" (Gen. 1:1). And then I read verse 16, the greatest understatement ever: "He made the stars also" (NASB). A universe one hundred billion light-years across, containing countless trillions of stars, and the Bible makes them sound like a casual add-on!

I quickly realized this book is about a Person who made the celestial heavens—including that great galaxy of Andromeda, and the earth—and me.

Because I had no reference points when I read the Bible, it wasn't just Leviticus that confused me. But when I reached the Gospels, everything changed. I was fascinated by Jesus.

At first, I thought Jesus was fiction—a superhero like in the comics. But everything about Jesus had the ring of truth. Then I realized something incredible. While reading the Bible, I had come to believe Jesus is real. By a miracle of grace, he transformed my life.

Discovering Lewis

I was hungry for truth, so I regularly visited a Christian bookstore, which featured thousands of spine-out books in the remodeled garage of a private home. One day I came across a book called *The Problem of Pain*. It was my first encounter with C. S. Lewis.

I was stunned by his insight and clarity. He remembered what it was like not to know God, just like I did. He spoke of longing, like mine. I went back to the store and found Lewis's space trilogy: *Out of the Silent Planet*; *Perelandra*; and *That Hideous Strength*.

My church left me with the impression that using my imagination might be a sin, so I'd assumed science fiction was a thing of the past. Yet this same author with the great insights had also exercised his imagination by creating engaging science fiction. *Perelandra* contained deep theology, with Maleldil and the oyarsa, the Green Lady, and Ransom, the Christ type, fighting Weston, the Unman and Devil figure. I was transported to another world while taken deep into the gospel itself, and I ate it up.

My telescope had sat unused for years. After reading Lewis's space trilogy, I went outside and once more gazed at the galaxy of Andromeda. Again I wept. But this time for a very different reason: gratitude. Now I knew personally the God who had spun into being the trillion stars and countless planets of the Andromeda galaxy and the Milky Way.

Sure, I was still small, but I'd met the one who is infinitely big. Finally, I knew whom to worship. I was on the inside, not the outside. I was no longer the star of a pitiful little drama about me; I was a role player, a character actor in a story of infinite greatness.

Then I read the Chronicles of Narnia. Truth leapt at me from every page. In *The Lion, the Witch and the Wardrobe* I read, "[Aslan is] not like a *tame* lion.[1] . . . [Aslan] isn't safe. But he's GOOD!"[2]

In *The Silver Chair* I read about Jill Pole. Desperate to quench her thirst, she wanted the lion to promise he wouldn't eat her if she came to drink. When he refused, she determined to find another stream. Even though I'd been a Christian only a short while, when Aslan said, "There is no other stream," I knew exactly what he meant. And when I see God at work, I still sometimes repeat words from Narnia: "Aslan is on the move."

In *Prince Caspian* I read a hundred pages of theology poured into two sentences: "You come of the Lord Adam and the Lady Eve," said Aslan. "And that is both honour enough to erect the head of the poorest beggar, and shame enough to bow the shoulders of the greatest emperor on earth."[3]

Time and time again, Lewis's theology stunned me. Lucy tells Aslan that he looks bigger than before, and Aslan says, "Every year you grow, you will find me bigger."[4] I did then and I do now still find the never-changing God to be ever-bigger in my eyes.

---

[1] C. S. Lewis, *The Lion, the Witch and the Wardrobe* (New York: HarperCollins, 1978), 200 (emphasis original).
[2] Ibid., 86 (emphasis added).
[3] C. S. Lewis, *Prince Caspian* (New York: HarperCollins, 1979), 233.
[4] Ibid., 148.

Tackling Tough Questions

Lewis was the first one to help me grapple with the big questions. In *The Problem of Pain*, he described how he used to argue against the Christian faith:

> Not many years ago when I was an atheist, if anyone had asked me, "Why do you not believe in God?" my reply would have [been]: "Look at the universe we live in." . . . History is largely a record of crime, war, disease, and terror. . . . The universe . . . is running down. . . . All stories will come to nothing: all life will turn out in the end to have been a transitory and senseless contortion upon the idiotic face of infinite matter. If you ask me to believe that this is the work of a benevolent and omnipotent spirit, I reply that all the evidence points in the opposite direction. Either there is no spirit behind the universe, or else a spirit indifferent to good and evil, or else an evil spirit.[5]

I loved that Lewis clearly articulated the problem of evil and suffering better than most atheists, including Richard Dawkins. Yet he embraced a biblical worldview that had a far greater explanatory power than his atheism. And he passed it on to me and countless others.

Young people go to college unprepared intellectually for what they'll face. Let's feed them C. S. Lewis on evil and suffering before they hear the rants of atheist and agnostic college professors, most of them intellectual pygmies compared to Lewis. Let's not leave it to the world to ask the hard questions—the Bible raises these very questions and answers them better than any other worldview. It was Lewis who first showed me that.

No Stranger to Suffering

A few years ago, I reread *The Problem of Pain* and *A Grief Observed*, one right after the other. *The Problem of Pain* is more reasoned and logical, while *A Grief Observed* contains raw suffering as Lewis expresses

---

[5] C. S. Lewis, *The Problem of Pain* (New York: Macmillan, 1962), 13–15.

overwhelming grief after the death of his wife, Joy. The books are supplementary but, given their contexts, not contradictory.

There are two movies about C. S. Lewis named *Shadowlands*. They're both good productions, but the BBC version is generally more accurate. In the Hollywood version, Lewis is played by Anthony Hopkins. The movie portrays Lewis as an ivory-tower professor who knew little of suffering. Then when his wife, Joy, dies of cancer, it portrays him as doubting the supposedly superficial things he'd written in *The Problem of Pain*. At the movie's end, Lewis sits down in the attic next to his young stepson, Douglas Gresham. The real-life Doug Gresham is my friend, and we've discussed this false portrayal of Lewis.

In *Surprised by Joy* Lewis tells of his mother's death when he was nine: "With my mother's death all settled happiness, all that was tranquil and reliable, disappeared from my life. There was to be . . . no more of the old security. It was sea and islands now; the great continent, like Atlantis, had slid under the waves."[6]

He was alienated from his disapproving father and abused by bullies in his boarding schools, one with a headmaster declared insane. On the battlefields of World War I, Lewis was hit by shrapnel in three places, one piece so close to his heart that it was never removed. By age nineteen he'd seen countless friends slaughtered in battle. For years, Doug Gresham says, Lewis suffered terrible nightmares about being back in the trenches.[7]

Though Lewis was phenomenally popular with students, it troubled him that his Oxford College, Magdalen, snubbed him by never granting him a full professorship or an academic chair. It was Oxford's rival, Cambridge University, that offered him in 1954 the chair of medieval and Renaissance literature. His peers at Oxford resented his faith and were embarrassed by or jealous of his popularity among the masses (those *ordinary* people).

---

[6] C. S. Lewis, *Surprised by Joy: The Shape of My Early Life* (New York: Harcourt Brace Jovanovich, 1955), 21.

[7] Douglas H. Gresham, *Jack's Life: The Life Story of C. S. Lewis* (Nashville, TN: Broadman, 2005), 158.

Lewis spent many years caring for Mrs. Moore, the demanding and critical mother of a friend who had died in the war. The daily burdens of letter writing, various ailments, and his brother Warnie's alcoholism took a heavy toll on him.

Many Christians see God from a prosperity-theology perspective. When suffering comes, they believe God has failed them. But God's love and goodness do not mean life will go as we want! Have you noticed that? Lewis did. *The Problem of Pain* is certainly not naïve. Lewis said,

> God, who has made us, knows what we are and that our happiness lies in Him. Yet we will not seek it in Him as long as He leaves us any other resort where it can even plausibly be looked for. While what we call "our own life" remains agreeable we will not surrender it to Him. What then can God do in our interests but make "our own life" less agreeable to us, and take away the plausible sources of false happiness?[8]

Lewis asked, "What do people mean when they say 'I am not afraid of God because I know He is good'? Have they never even been to a dentist?"[9]

Suffering can be the road to transforming grace. Lewis walked that road. When Joy's cancer was taking its toll, Lewis wrote to a friend, "We are not necessarily doubting that God will do the best for us. We are wondering how painful the best will turn out to be."[10]

Heaven: God's Answer to Suffering

Paul captured the eternal remedy to evil and suffering in Romans 8:18: "I consider that the sufferings of this present time are not worth comparing with the glory that is to be revealed to us." After citing Romans 8:18 in *The Problem of Pain*, Lewis says that "a book on suffering which says nothing of heaven, is leaving out almost the whole

---

[8] Lewis, *The Problem of Pain*, 96–97.
[9] C. S. Lewis, *A Grief Observed* (Kent, UK: Whitstable Litho, 1966), 36.
[10] C. S. Lewis, *Letters of C. S. Lewis* (Orlando, FL: Harcourt, 1966), 477.

of one side of the account. Scripture and tradition habitually put the joys of heaven into the scale against the sufferings of earth, and no solution of the problem of pain which does not do so can be called a Christian one."[11]

He's absolutely right. Strangely, there are Christian books on evil and suffering which say almost nothing about heaven. But present sufferings *must* be seen in light of the promise of eternal happiness in God. The scales can't be balanced in this life alone.

Paul says in 2 Corinthians 4:17, "This light momentary affliction is preparing for us an eternal weight of glory beyond all comparison." Read 2 Corinthians 11:24–28 for a record of Paul's "light" and "momentary" affliction:

> Five times I received at the hands of the Jews the forty lashes less one. Three times I was beaten with rods. Once I was stoned. Three times I was shipwrecked; a night and a day I was adrift at sea; on frequent journeys, in danger from rivers, danger from robbers, danger from my own people, danger from Gentiles, danger in the city, danger in the wilderness, danger at sea, danger from false brothers; in toil and hardship, through many a sleepless night, in hunger and thirst, often without food, in cold and exposure. And, apart from other things, there is the daily pressure on me of my anxiety for all the churches.

For Paul to call these "light" and "momentary" says a great deal about the glory he was comparing them to. Indeed, some suffering weighs so heavily—holocausts, rape, human trafficking, torture, children dying of leukemia and starvation—that what fills the *other* side of the scales must be weighty beyond all comprehension. And it is: eternal happiness and worshiping and serving the King of kings as resurrected people on a resurrected earth.

No wonder Satan, the liar, seeks to deceive us about heaven and the resurrection. If he convinces us that eternity will be boring, spent

---

[11] Lewis, *The Problem of Pain*, 144.

floating on clouds, then we'll waste this life, thinking it is our only chance to experience happiness.

Ironically, in a day when people edit theology to fit their desires, we ignore biblical truths about eternity that are far more desirable than what we falsely believe. Shouldn't we embrace the true biblical teaching of the resurrection and the new earth and let ourselves and our children be excited about them?

Look at Romans 8.

"For the creation waits with eager longing for the revealing of the sons of God" (v. 19). Everywhere you look, you can sense something has gone terribly wrong. Yet we know something good is coming.

"For the creation was subjected to futility . . . in hope" (v. 20). As the human stewards of earth fell, all creation fell with them. This is the curse. As Adam's descendants, we're left with a nostalgia for the Eden we've never known yet that somehow circulates in our blood.

". . . that the creation itself will be set free from its bondage to corruption and obtain the freedom of the glory of the children of God" (v. 21). Not just any hope but a blood-bought certainty. The same creation that fell on humanity's coattails shall rise on its coattails.

"For we know that the whole creation has been groaning together in the pains of childbirth until now" (v. 22). This is the birth pangs of new life. Notice that Paul says "whole creation." What else besides mankind is groaning? Figuratively, forests and meadows and mountains. Literally, suffering animals.

"And not only the creation, but we ourselves, who have the firstfruits of the Spirit, groan inwardly as we wait eagerly for adoption as sons, the redemption of our bodies" (v. 23).

Resurrection is the hinge on which the problem of suffering turns. This is a groaning creation, we are groaning people and the Holy Spirit himself intercedes for us with groanings (v. 26). God does not minimize or deny suffering. He tackles it head-on in perhaps the most triumphant chapter in the Bible.

Think again of 2 Corinthians 4:17. It says that eternal glory far outweighs our worst suffering. It's not that temporary suffering is so *small*; it's that eternal glory is so *huge*. Your suffering may be a boulder the size of the Rock of Gibraltar. But suppose you put that rock on one side of the scales, then on the other side you put the planet Jupiter. In and of themselves our sufferings may be weighty, but compare them to eternal glory, everlasting happiness, endless beauty, and unbroken relationships. The relative weights change our perspective, don't they?

Our Resurrection: Key to Creation's Redemption

God never gave up his plans for us and for the earth. Not only will our bodies rise, but earth itself will be reborn and become all God intended it to be.

How far will redemption reach? Isaac Watts, a great hymn writer and an accomplished theologian, nailed it in *Joy to the World*: "Far as the curse is found." God's redemptive plan includes all the groaning creation—people and animals. God will not abandon his creation; he will redeem it. He doesn't give up on the earth any more than he gives up on us. Righteous humanity will indeed rule the earth to the glory of God—forever.

Second Peter 3:13 says, "According to his promise we are waiting for new heavens and a new earth in which righteousness dwells." Even if we weren't told about the new earth, we would have to deduce it, because physically resurrected bodies need somewhere physical to live. A new car is still a car. A new body is still a body. A new earth is still an earth. "New" is the adjective, "earth" the noun. The noun is the thing. God wouldn't call it the *new* earth if it were not a *real* earth.

One of the greatest gifts we can give our children and grandchildren is to teach them the doctrines of the resurrection and the new earth. They need to know they are made for a person and a place. *Jesus* is the person. *Heaven* is the place—not a ghostly place but God's central dwelling place, which he promises to relocate to the new earth.

A man I met years ago told me, "I love God. But the truth is, I want to live with Jesus forever *on this earth*, without all the sin and suffering." What he longed for is exactly what God has promised. Don't try to get children excited about becoming ghosts. They're no more capable of wanting that than of developing an appetite for gravel. God has made us to be physical beings living in a physical world—eating, drinking, playing, working, loving, and laughing to God's glory. That's the promise of resurrection.

Lewis wrote, "There have been times when I think we do not desire heaven but more often I find myself wondering whether, in our heart of hearts, we have ever desired anything else."[12] This is true, and yet it is heaven *on earth* we long for, isn't it?

The problem with earth is not its physicality. Earth's problem is sin and the curse. We long for a repaired earth, where God's glorious creation shines without the dark clouds of sin, death, and gloom. God made Adam *from* the earth and *for* the earth. He made humanity to rule it for his glory.

God made no mistake when he wired us for a physical existence. That's why the doctrine of the present heaven alone is an insufficient remedy for the problem of evil and suffering. A Platonic disembodied state could never counterbalance or compensate for present sufferings. Paul says, "If in Christ we have hope *in this life only*, we are of all people most to be pitied" (1 Cor. 15:19). Physical suffering on earth can't be rectified by a disembodied existence in a netherworld. Those are apples and oranges. Romans 8 is about apples and apples, a suffering life on earth remedied by a glorious new life with new bodies on a new earth.

Redemption is not escape from earthly life. It is reclamation of earthly life. When Jesus died, God wasn't done with his old body. His resurrection body was his old body made new. God is not done with these bodies or this earth. Our old bodies will be made new, and this old earth will be made new.

---

[12] Ibid., 144–48.

Turning Bad into Best

In Romans 8:28, Paul wrote, "We know that for those who love God all things work together for good." This verse tells us what we will one day see in retrospect.

Lewis, in *The Great Divorce*, wrote that "both good and evil, when they are full grown, become retrospective. . . . Heaven, once attained, will work backwards and turn even that agony into a glory."[13]

The curse will be reversed. Lewis has Aslan explain the deeper magic the witch didn't know about when he died for a sinner: "The Table would crack and Death itself would start working backward."[14]

Retrospect enables us to see everything differently. It's why we can call the worst day in all of history "Good Friday."

Faith is like a forward memory, allowing us to believe as if what is promised has already happened. One day we will see how Romans 8:28 was true all along, even in those moments we most doubted it. Joseph saw this in Genesis 50:20, the Romans 8:28 of the Old Testament: "You meant evil against me, but God meant it for good." (Notice Joseph didn't merely say, "God made the best of bad circumstances.")

Here's a question: How long will it take living with God on the new earth before you say, "At last, all that suffering was worth it"? Five seconds? Five minutes? Five years? Maybe you're a pessimist, and you think, "It would take five hundred years before it would be worth it." Well, fine, Eeyore, or perhaps I should say Puddleglum; after five hundred years you'll have an eternity of unending, God-centered happiness in front of you, paid for by the shed blood of God. Can you think of *anything* better?

There is only one answer bigger than the question of evil and suffering: *Jesus.* Do you ever think, *I would never do to my child what God has done to me! He must not care?* Picture Jesus stretching his nail-scarred hands toward you and asking, "Do these look like the hands

---

[13] C. S. Lewis, *The Great Divorce* (San Francisco, CA: HarperSanFrancisco, 1946), 69.
[14] C. S. Lewis, *The Lion, the Witch and the Wardrobe* (New York: HarperCollins, 1994), 94.

of a God who does not care?" God's Son, by taking upon himself our sins, suffered far more than any person in history.

If God decided all the suffering of history is worth the price paid, who are we to say otherwise? He knows everything and took upon himself the lion's share of human suffering. Hasn't he earned the right to be trusted?

Take some time to list the worst things that have ever happened to you, then list the best things. You'll be astonished by how many of those best things came out of the worst things. Trust God to do the same with things that don't yet make sense. In the hands of a God of sovereign grace, our sufferings will give birth to future happiness beyond our wildest dreams. Jesus said our sorrows will turn into joy—not just be followed by joy but transformed into joy (John 16:20). Think of it: for God's children, what is now pain will ultimately be transfigured into both glory and joy.

A Closer Look at Lewis and the New Earth

There is much to look forward to about being with Christ in the present heaven. As Paul put it, to be absent from the body is to be present with the Lord (2 Cor. 5:8).

Lewis wrote to a believing American woman who thought she was dying:

> Can you not see death as a friend and deliverer? . . . What is there to be afraid of? . . . Your sins are confessed. . . . Has this world been so kind to you that you should leave with regret? There are better things ahead than any we leave behind. . . . Our Lord says to you, "Peace, child, peace. Relax. Let go. I will catch you."[15]

Lewis added, "Of course, this may not be the end. Then make it a good rehearsal." He signed the letter, "Yours (and like you, a tired traveler, near the journey's end)." Five months later, he died.

Colossians 3 commands us to think about the present heaven,

---

[15] C. S. Lewis, *Letters to an American Lady* (Grand Rapids, MI: Eerdmans, 1967), 117.

where Christ is seated at God's right hand. But Scripture is also clear that the heaven that should most dominate our thinking is the eternal kingdom of God, the climactic culmination of God's unfolding drama of redemption.

"But in keeping with his promise we are looking forward to a new heaven and a new earth, where righteousness dwells" (2 Pet. 3:13 NIV). But how can we look forward to it if we don't think about it? And how can we think about it unless we are taught about it from God's Word? Suppose a trip awaits you, and you will be flying from Miami to Santa Barbara, with a layover in Dallas. Dallas is not your final destination. You say, "I'm headed to Santa Barbara." Or at most you say, "I'm headed to Santa Barbara by way of Dallas." According to Scripture, the new earth is our final destination. The present heaven will be a stop along the way toward resurrection. (It'll be a *wonderful* layover. In Philippians 1:23 Paul calls it "far better" than our present existence; infinitely better than the Dallas airport.)

Revelation 21:1–4 beautifully portrays what awaits God's children:

> Then I saw a new heaven and a new earth, for the first heaven and the first earth had passed away. And I saw the holy city, new Jerusalem, coming down out of heaven from God. . . . And I heard a loud voice from the throne saying, "Behold, the dwelling place of God is with man. He will dwell with them, and they will be his people, and God himself will be with them as their God. He will wipe away every tear from their eyes, and death shall be no more, neither shall there be mourning, nor crying, nor pain anymore, for the former things have passed away."

Multiple times in that passage God says he will come down from the present heaven to live with his people on the new earth. The city comes down out of heaven, God's dwelling place is "with man," God will "dwell with them," and "God himself will be with them." Despite the repetition, most Christians still don't appear to believe that God's plan *is* to bring heaven to earth and dwell here with us forever. Not just for a thousand years in a millennial kingdom on the old earth, but *forever* on the new earth. Christ is Emmanuel, "God with us," forever. The incarnation of Jesus was not temporary.

We normally think of our going up to heaven to live with God in his place. That is indeed what happens when we die. But the ultimate promise is that *God will come down to live with us in our place*, on the new earth. The ultimate heaven will not be "us with God" but God with us (Rev. 21:3).

I love Lewis's valiant mouse, Reepicheep, who single-mindedly sought Aslan's country: "While I can, I sail east in the *Dawn Treader*. When she fails me, I paddle east in my coracle. When she sinks, I shall swim east with my four paws. And when I can swim no longer, if I have not reached Aslan's country, or shot over the edge of the world in some vast cataract, I shall sink with my nose to the sunrise."[16]

Reepicheep doesn't long for Aslan's "Ghostly Realm of Cloudy Nothingness." He longs to be with his king forever in that solid country with land, mountains, rivers, metals, plains, trees, animals, and people with physical bodies. The ground quakes under Aslan as he prowls. Aslan is real and tangible, and his flowing mane can be touched if you dare. Reepicheep loves Aslan not as a disembodied spirit but as a tangible mighty lion; king of kings; ruler of Narnia, earth, and all worlds. Reepicheep longs to be in Aslan's country, for he longs for Aslan himself.

We want Jesus, so naturally we should want to live where he lives. Hebrews 11:16 says, "They desire a better country, that is, a heavenly one." The patriarchs longed for a better country because they longed for God. The reason heaven matters is that God lives there.

In *Mere Christianity* Lewis lamented that we haven't been trained to want heaven:

> Our whole education tends to fix our minds on this world. . . .
> When the real want for Heaven is present in us, we do not recog-
> nize it. Most people, if they had really learned to look into their

---

[16] C. S. Lewis, *The Voyage of the Dawn Treader* (New York: Scholastic, 1952), 24.

own hearts, would know that they do want, and want acutely,
something that cannot be had in this world. There are all sorts
of things in this world that offer to give it to you, but they never
quite keep their promise. . . . If we find ourselves with a desire that
nothing in this world can satisfy, the most probable explanation
is that we were made for another world.[17]

Heaven's Physical Side

People have told me that a physical earth and resurrection bodies
and eating and drinking sounds "unspiritual." Lewis says in *Mere
Christianity*:

> There is no use trying to be more spiritual than God. God never
> meant man to be a purely spiritual creature. . . . He likes matter.
> He invented it.[18]

And:

> Christianity is almost the only one of the great religions which
> thoroughly approves of the body—which believes that matter is
> good, that God Himself once took on a human body, and that
> some kind of body is going to be given to us even in Heaven and
> is going to be an essential part of our happiness, our beauty, and
> our energy.[19]

In *The Four Loves* Lewis refers to redeemed relationships and culture: "We may hope that the resurrection of the body means also the
resurrection of what may be called our 'greater body'; the general
fabric of our earthly life with its affections and relationships."[20]

Isaiah 60 and 65 along with Revelation 21 and 22 say about the
new earth that the kings of the earth will bring their glory into the
New Jerusalem, and its gates will never be shut. They will bring into

---

[17] C. S. Lewis, *Mere Christianity* (New York: Macmillan, 1960), 119.
[18] C. S. Lewis, *Mere Christianity* (New York: HarperCollins, 1952), 65.
[19] Ibid., 99.
[20] C. S. Lewis, *The Four Loves* (New York: Harcourt Brace Jovanovich, 1960), 187.

it the splendors and the honor of the nations (see Isa. 60:3; Rev. 21:21–25). What splendors? Tributes to the King of kings.

There is nothing more solid, more earthly, and less ghostly than city walls made of rocks and precious stones. If there will be redeemed architecture, music, and art, why not science, technology, play, writing, reading, and exploration—all done to the glory of God? We're told, "His servants will worship him" (Rev. 22:3). We'll have meaningful work serving our King. And we will enjoy rest and relaxation (Heb. 4:1–11; Rev. 14:13).

Will we eat and drink in the resurrection? Scripture couldn't be more emphatic (Matt. 8:11; Rev. 2:7; 19:9). Jesus said, "People will come from east and west, and from north and south, and recline at table in the kingdom of God" (Luke 13:29). Isaiah 25:6 says, "On this mountain the LORD of hosts will make for all peoples a feast of rich food, a feast of well-aged wine." How good a meal will that be? My compliments to the chef—the Lord God.

The bucket-list mentality reveals an impoverished view of redemption. Even Christians end up thinking, *If I can't live my dreams now, I never will.* Or, *You only go around once.* But if you know Jesus, you go around twice—and the second time lasts forever. It's called "eternal life," and it will be lived in a redeemed universe with King Jesus.

We do not pass our peaks in this life. The best is yet to come. Missed opportunities will be replaced by billions of new and better opportunities—some graciously granted us by God as rewards for our faithfulness now. Don't wait until you die to believe that. Believing it *now* will change how you think, how you view the people around you, and what you do with your time and money, which are really God's.

I am convinced that the typical view of heaven—eternity in a disembodied state—is not only completely contrary to the Bible but obscures the far richer truth: that God promises us eternal life as totally healthy, embodied people *more* capable of worship, friendship, love, discovery, work, and play than we have ever been.

Continuity

Sadly, there are Christians who would die rather than deny the doctrine of the resurrection yet who don't *believe* what resurrection actually means—that we'll live forever as physical beings in a redeemed physical world. This is *amazingly* good news—the very thing we long for.

The risen Christ said, "See my hands and my feet, that it is I myself. Touch me, and see. For a spirit does not have flesh and bones" (Luke 24:39). The scars testified that his new body was the same old body made new. Likewise, we will be ourselves when we are raised. Without continuity between the old and the new, resurrection would not be resurrection.

Philippians 3:20–21 says, "But our citizenship is in heaven, and from it we await a Savior, the Lord Jesus Christ, who will transform our lowly body to be like his glorious body, by the power that enables him even to subject all things to himself." Christ declared his resurrection body to be flesh and bones. Ours will be too.

The 1646 Westminster Confession says, "All the dead shall be raised up, with the self-same bodies, and none other." This is continuity. So was what Job said in his suffering: "I know that my Redeemer lives, and at the last he will stand upon the earth. [Not heaven, but earth.] And after my skin has been thus destroyed, yet in my flesh I shall see God, whom I shall see for myself, and my eyes shall behold, and not another" (Job 19:25–27).

It will really be Job. It was really Jesus. And it will really be us. Help your children not to be afraid of heaven. Teach them what resurrection and continuity mean. *Of course* they will remain themselves in heaven. Of course they will remember who they are and who their family and friends are. When we stand before God and give an account of our whole lives (2 Cor. 5:10), our memories will have to be far *better*, not worse.

When I came to Christ, I became a new person (2 Cor. 5:17), but my dog didn't bark at me, and my mother didn't call the police and say, "My son has been taken over by aliens." I was the same me made new. Transformation and continuity are not contradictions. New people are old people made new. New bodies are old bodies made new, and the new earth will be the old earth made new.

Why the Silence?

I went to a fine Bible college and seminary, but in my classes we *never* talked about the new earth. In eschatology class, we devoted weeks to different views of the rapture. We talked about the return of Christ and the millennium, but our discussions of Revelation involved so much talk about the Antichrist that we never reached Revelation 21 and 22, which are all about the new heavens and new earth, where we will live forever with God and our spiritual family, worshiping and serving him in eternal happiness, for his everlasting glory. (That's a pretty conspicuous omission, if you think about it.) By the time I became a pastor, I had thought through nearly every major doctrine of Scripture but had given no thought whatsoever to where I will spend eternity, in the new heavens and new earth.

William Shedd's three-volume *Dogmatic Theology* contains eighty-seven pages on eternal punishment, but only two on heaven.[21] In his nine-hundred-page theology, *Great Doctrines of the Bible*, Martyn Lloyd-Jones devotes less than two pages to the eternal state and the new earth.[22]

Louis Berkhof's classic *Systematic Theology* devotes thirty-eight pages to creation, forty pages to baptism and Communion, and fifteen pages to what theologians call "the intermediate state" (where people live between death and resurrection). Yet it contains only two pages on hell and just one page on the new heavens and new earth.

When all that's said about the eternal heaven is limited to page 737 of a 737-page systematic theology like Berkhof's (and an excellent one at that), it raises a question: Does Scripture really have so little

---

[21] W. G. T. Shedd, *Dogmatic Theology*, 3 vols. (Grand Rapids, MI: Zondervan, n.d.).
[22] D. Martyn Lloyd-Jones, *Great Doctrines of the Bible*, vol. 3, *The Church and the Last Things* (Wheaton, IL: Crossway, 2003), 246–48.

to say about the resurrected world where we will live forever? (If Shedd, Lloyd-Jones, and Berkhof had done no more than quote the biblical texts from Isaiah 60; 65; 66; Ezekiel 48; Daniel 7; 2 Peter 3; and Revelation 21–22, without a single comment, the space used to treat this subject would have quadrupled.)

The doctrine of the new heavens and new earth is not some late-developing afterthought but a central component of redemptive history and intention. If you've never studied these biblical doctrines, I encourage you to. It will revolutionize your thinking. Small views of God's redemptive work produce small views of God. The redemptive story of God's work on earth is powerful, so let's not shrink it.

As theologian Greg Beale puts it, "New creation is the New Testament's hermeneutical and eschatological center of gravity."[23] He says this is "the dominating notion of biblical theology because new creation is the goal or purpose of God's redemptive-historical plan; new creation is the logical main point of Scripture."[24]

Making All Things New

Jesus said, "At the renewal of *all* things, when the Son of Man sits on his glorious throne, you who have followed me will also sit on twelve thrones, judging the twelve tribes" (Matt. 19:28 NIV). Renewal is one of many *re-* words in the Bible: redemption, regeneration, restoration, reconciliation, resurrection—words that speak of reclaiming what was lost.

In *Creation Regained* Albert Wolters wrote,

God hangs on to his fallen original creation and salvages it. He refuses to abandon the work of his hands—in fact, he sacrifices his own Son to save his original project. Humankind, which has botched its original mandate . . . is given another chance in Christ; we are reinstated as God's managers on earth.[25]

---

[23] Greg K. Beale, "The Eschatological Conception of New Testament Theology," in *Eschatology in Bible and Theology*, ed. Kent E. Brower and Mark W. Elliott (Downers Grove, IL: InterVarsity, 1997), 50.
[24] Ibid., 21–22.
[25] Albert M. Wolters, *Creation Regained* (Grand Rapids, MI: Eerdmans, 1985), 58.

What do we find in the last two chapters of the Bible? A return to the first two chapters, only far more and far better. The river of the water of life, flowing from the throne of God, and the tree of life, now a forest of life, growing on both sides of the river (Rev. 21:1–2). That's a picture of the New Eden, located in the heart of the New Jerusalem.

In Genesis, the Redeemer is promised; in Revelation, the Redeemer returns. Genesis tells the story of Paradise lost; Revelation tells the story of Paradise regained. In Genesis, man and woman fail as earth's rulers; in Revelation righteous humanity rules the new earth, under King Jesus. Satan and sin will not thwart God's plan!

In Acts 3:21 Peter said that Christ must remain in heaven until the time comes for God to restore everything, as he promised long ago through his holy prophets. What does it mean that one day God will restore everything? Read the prophets: you'll see how God promises to restore earth itself to Eden-like conditions (Isa. 35:1; 51:3; 55:13; Ezek. 36:35).

In *Letters to Malcolm* Lewis wrote, "I can now communicate to you the fields of my boyhood—they are building-estates today—only imperfectly, by words. Perhaps the day is coming when I can take you for a walk through them."[26]

Home, but Far Better

When I came to Christ, we sang a song in my church: "This world is not my home, I'm just a passin' through." Well, this world as it is *now*, under the curse, isn't my home. But this world, in its redeemed form, *will* be my home forever.

Though Lewis makes new-earth allusions here and there in his nonfiction, he gives the most remarkable portrayal of the new earth in *The Last Battle*, the final Narnia book. We identify with Jewel the unicorn's lament over Narnia: "The only world I've ever known."

---

[26] C. S. Lewis, *Letters to Malcolm: Chiefly on Prayer* (New York: Harcourt Brace Jovanovich, 1963), 121–22.

This is the only world *we've* ever known. Lucy also grieves that Narnia has ended. Then she realizes what she's seeing:

> "Those hills," said Lucy, "the nice woody ones and the blue ones behind—aren't they very like the southern border of Narnia?"
>
> "Like!?" cried Edmund after a moment's silence. "Why they're *exactly* like. Look, there's Mount Pire with his forked head, and there's the pass into Archenland and everything!"
>
> "And yet . . . ," said Lucy. "They're different. They have more colours on them and they look further away than I remembered and they're more . . ."
>
> "More like the real thing," said the Lord Digory softly.
>
> Suddenly Farsight the Eagle spread his wings, soared thirty or forty feet up into the air, circled round and then alighted on the ground.
>
> "Kings and Queens," he cried, "we have all been blind. We are only beginning to see where we are. From up there I have seen it all—Ettinsmuir, Beaversdam, the Great River, and Cair Paravel still shining on the edge of the Eastern Sea. *Narnia is not dead. This is Narnia.*"[27]

Lewis reflects beautifully the biblical truth of the new earth:

> "The Eagle is right," said the Lord Digory. "The Narnia you're thinking of . . . was only a shadow or a copy of the real Narnia, which has always been here and always will be here: just as our own world, England and all, is only a shadow or copy of something in Aslan's real world. *You need not mourn over Narnia, Lucy.* All of the old Narnia that mattered, all the dear creatures, have been drawn into the real Narnia through the Door. And of course it is different; as different as a real thing is from a shadow or as waking life is from a dream." . . .
>
> The new [Narnia] was a deeper country: every rock and flower and blade of grass looked as if it meant more. I can't de-

---

[27] C. S. Lewis, *The Last Battle* (New York: Collier, 1956), 168–71 (emphases added).

scribe it any better than that: if you ever get there, you will know what I mean. It was the Unicorn who summed up what everyone was feeling. He . . . cried: "I have come home at last! *This is my real country!* I belong here. This is the land I have been looking for all my life, though I never knew it till now. The reason why we loved the old Narnia is that it sometimes looked a little like this."[28]

Will the new earth be different? Of course—just as we will be different. Still us, but far better. On the new earth we will say, "The reason we loved the old earth is that sometimes it looked a little like this." And we will say, like the unicorn, "Come further up, come further in!"[29]

Our children and grandchildren love adventures. Let's tell them eternity will be the great adventure that never ends. And if they don't see and do everything they want in this life, no worries; they'll live forever on the new earth that's way better, without sin, suffering, war, sorrow, and death.

Eustace is puzzled because "we saw it all destroyed and the sun put out."[30] Yes, the old Narnia was destroyed, but this is the resurrected Narnia. Likewise people say, "But 2 Peter 3:10–12 says the earth will be destroyed." Of course. Death always precedes resurrection. "The new earth" doesn't mean earth doesn't die but rather that after dying it is raised. It may seem impossible to us, but it's simple to God.

When the children see Professor Kirk's home where they first entered the wardrobe, Edmund says, "I thought that house had been destroyed." The faun, Tumnus, answers that it was, "but you are now looking at the England within England, the real England just as this is the real Narnia. And in that inner England no good thing is destroyed."[31]

---

[28] Ibid. (emphases added).
[29] Ibid., 161–62.
[30] Ibid., 169.
[31] Ibid., 168–71.

Taste and See

God is not done with this earth. He promises a new earth with a new Jerusalem. Why not other cities made new (as in Jesus saying, "You are to be over five cities," in Luke 19:19)? Why not a new Ireland, where Lewis might take us for a walk through his boyhood fields? Or maybe we'll go back in time for that. Why not a new Niagara Falls, a new Lake Victoria, a new Grand Canyon, a redeemed Nairobi, a glorified Seattle?

It was no accident that Jesus was a carpenter. Carpenters make things and fix things. The carpenter from Nazareth made the universe, and he's going to fix it. God is the ultimate salvage artist. And what he restores will be far better than the original. He delights in that, and we should delight in him.

In *The Weight of Glory* Lewis said,

> The faint, far-off results of those energies which God's creative rapture implanted in matter when He made the worlds are what we now call physical pleasures; and even thus filtered, they are too much for our present management. What would it be to taste at the fountainhead that stream of which even these lower reaches prove so intoxicating? Yet that, I believe, is what lies before us. The whole man is to drink joy from the fountain of joy.[32]

The best we enjoy here—great food, relationships, worship, and culture—is a mere foretaste of what awaits us on the new earth, where we'll be without sin and death and curse. In that world we will always see that God himself is the fountainhead of joy.

No More Death Means No More Sin

Believers who think heaven will be boring show that they think God is boring. Hell will be boring. Heaven will be the ultimate adventure, because God is the ultimate adventure. We'll never exhaust him. Paul says in Ephesians 2:7, "In the coming ages [God will] show the

---

[32] C. S. Lewis, *The Weight of Glory* (New York: Macmillan, 1980), 17–18.

immeasurable riches of his grace in kindness toward us in Christ Jesus."

Revelation 22:3–4 says, "No longer will there be anything accursed, but the throne of God and of the Lamb will be in it, and his servants will worship him. They will see his face. . . . And they will *reign* forever and ever."

Seeing God is what the ancients called the "beatific vision." That literally means, "The happy-making sight." To see God will be to experience undiminished happiness. When we feel like saying, "It doesn't get any better than this," it will.

Psalm 16:11 says: "In your presence there is fullness of joy; at your right hand are pleasures forevermore." Who needs a bucket list? The blood-bought promise of the gospel is this: we *will* live happily ever after—with God, the source of all happiness.

Will there be a second fall in the eternal state? Absolutely not. We will have the righteousness of Christ. Sin? Been there. Done that. The illusion of its appeal will be gone.

Lewis portrays it like this in *The Last Battle*:

> Everyone raised his hand to pick the fruit he best liked the look of, and then everyone paused for a second. This fruit was so beautiful that each felt, "It can't be meant for me . . . surely we're not allowed to pluck it."
>
> "It's all right," said Peter. ". . . I've a feeling we've got to the country where everything is allowed."[33]

Happily Ever After

In the final chapter of *The Last Battle*, called "Farewell to Shadowlands," Aslan gives the children shocking news: "'There was a real railway accident,' said Aslan softly. 'Your father and mother and all of you are—as you used to call it in the Shadowlands—dead. The term is over: the holidays have begun. The dream is ended: this is the morning.'"[34]

---

[33] Lewis, *The Last Battle*, 137.
[34] Ibid., 183.

And as He spoke He no longer looked to them like a lion; but the things that began to happen after that were so great and beautiful that I cannot write them. And for us this is the end of all the stories, and we can most truly say that they all lived happily ever after. But for them it was only the beginning of the real story. All their life in this world and all their adventures in Narnia had *only been the cover and the title page*: now at last they were beginning Chapter One of the Great Story which no one on earth has read; which goes on forever; in which every chapter is better than the one before.[35]

Such is the vast and far-reaching redemptive plan of King Jesus.

Many nights I still look up at the Andromeda galaxy and still long to go there. Did God put that in my heart? When God creates the new heavens, might there be a new Andromeda galaxy? Or other new galaxies, nebulae, planets, moons, comets? Why not? Might we someday travel there to behold God's creative magnificence? If I do, my heart will be overwhelmed with praise to the God who redeemed not only that boy gazing through that telescope but also the great universe that first drew me to Christ with all its wonders.

---

[35] Ibid., 183–84 (emphasis added).

6

WHAT GOD MADE IS GOOD—AND MUST BE SANCTIFIED

C. S. Lewis and St. Paul on the Use of Creation

1 Timothy 4:1–5

JOHN PIPER

In the previous chapter, Randy Alcorn wrote that we will eat and drink in the new earth. He quoted C. S. Lewis that this is not unspiritual but designed by God. Here's the longer quote:

> There is no good trying to be more spiritual than God. God never meant man to be a purely spiritual creature. That is why he uses material things like bread and wine to put the new life into us. We may think this rather rude and unspiritual. God does not: he invented eating. He likes matter. He invented it.[1]

That's true. And my point in this chapter is that we don't have to wait for the new earth—we dare not wait for the new earth—to begin eating and drinking to the glory of God. I invite you to turn to 1 Timothy 4:1–5.

---

[1] C. S. Lewis, *Mere Christianity* (San Francisco: HarperCollins, 2001), 64.

Now the Spirit expressly says that in later times some will depart from the faith by devoting themselves to deceitful spirits and teachings of demons, through the insincerity of liars whose consciences are seared, who forbid marriage and require abstinence from foods that God created to be received with thanksgiving by those who believe and know the truth. For everything created by God is good, and nothing is to be rejected if it is received with thanksgiving, for it is made holy [sanctified] by the word of God and prayer.

Verses 1–3a describe the apostasy of people who are buying into demonic teachings about the evils of sex and food. Then in the middle of verse 3, Paul begins his response to these teachings and gives his positive alternative for the right use of creation—in particular, the right use of food, and by implication sex in marriage, and all other pleasures that come from this material world.

So let's look briefly at the demonic teachings of verses 1–3a and then focus most of our time on Paul's positive alternative, with C. S. Lewis giving insights along the way.

The Magnitude of This Issue

But first make sure you feel the magnitude of what we are dealing with here. The issue is: How are we to experience the material creation (which, of course, includes our bodies, and everything we encounter with our five senses) in such a way that God is worshiped, honored, loved, and supremely treasured in our experience of material creation?

You can feel the magnitude of this issue in two ways. First, as far as your daily experience goes, there is no more pervasive issue than this. And, second, as far as God's original purpose in creating the world goes, this issue is essential to that purpose.

Unlike many issues, this issue meets you every minute of your day—at least your waking day. In your waking hours, you are always seeing or hearing or smelling or tasting or touching some part of creation that is giving you some pleasure or pain, or something in between. And, therefore, the question of how this becomes part of your continual worship of God is pervasive.

And when God contemplated the creation of conscious human souls in addition to angels, he faced the question of whether these souls should be embodied, and whether they should live in a material universe, and how those bodies and that material world would accomplish his purposes to glorify himself in creation—because the Bible is unmistakably clear that the communication and exaltation of the glory of God is why God created the universe (Isa. 43:7; Col. 1:16; Eph. 1:6).

So I hope you feel some measure of the magnitude of the issue we are dealing with here in these verses in 1 Timothy. The Devil certainly feels the magnitude of what we are dealing with here, and he is behind the apostasy in the churches, especially in the last days, Paul says. Christians are leaving the faith, Paul says in verse 1 ("some will depart from the faith"). But they probably don't know they are leaving the faith. They think they are the truly faithful. We'll see this in a moment.

The Roots of the Apostasy

So let's look at the roots of this apostasy and see where it's coming from. The first source Paul mentions is "deceitful spirits." Verse 1: "Some will depart from the faith by devoting themselves to [or giving heed to, believing in] *deceitful spirits*." So the Devil and his demons are at work in the church to bring about this deception.

The apostle John calls Satan, in Revelation 12:9, "the deceiver of the whole world." And when John tackled the heresy of denying the physical incarnation of the Son of God, he said in 2 John 7, "Many deceivers have gone out into the world, those who do not confess the coming of Jesus Christ in the flesh. Such a one is the deceiver and the antichrist." So all along the way, leading to the last day, the deceiver is at work in the church.

Demonic Teachings

The second source of this apostasy is that these deceitful spirits produce teachings. They don't just work subconsciously in the mind or in the heart. They produce teachings in the church. Verse 1 at the end: "devoting themselves to deceitful spirits and *teachings of demons*." So there are teachings circulating in the churches to the effect that true godliness, or superior godliness, involves renouncing marriage and certain foods (v. 3).

Evidently the teaching of demons was that physical appetite for sex and physical appetite for food are defective. They are inferior to a kind of asceticism that sees in the physical world not God's ideal for us, but something second-class, something for the weak, who don't have the wherewithal to renounce sex and foods. This was not just a deceitful spirit but an actual teaching in the church that came, Paul said, from hell. It was demonic.

Coming through Real People

The third source of this apostasy was real people. Not just a spirit, and not just teachings, but people who were filled with this spirit and who advocated these teachings. Verses 1b–2: people were giving heed to deceitful spirits and teachings of demons "through the insincerity of liars whose consciences are seared."

The word "insincerity" is "hypocrisy" (Greek *hypocrisei*). In other words, these were professing Christians who presented themselves as teaching a higher godliness, but they were, Paul says, "false speakers" ("liars"). They may or may not have known they were speaking falsely. All we know is that they were teaching the teachings of demons and not the teachings of God. They were hypocrites. They presented themselves as one thing when in fact they were another thing, whether they knew it or not. Their consciences had been cauterized. Which may mean they were too callous to know they were speaking falsehood, or so callous they didn't care.

Satan's Deadly Subtlety

It seems to me, the most pressing question here is: Why would Satan seek to spread this kind of asceticism among the churches? At first glance, it seems odd to us. Isn't Satan's specialty, when it comes to sex, to entice people to want more, not less? Isn't pornography the issue today, not celibacy?

Isn't his specialty, when it comes to food, to entice people toward the destructive forces of gluttony and obesity, not toward moderation and abstinence? Doesn't Ephesians 2:1–3 describe our spiritual deadness in sin as "following the prince of the power of the air . . . *carrying out the desires of the body* . . . and by nature children of wrath"?

Oh, the subtlety of our great adversary! Of course, he wants you to do pornography and fornication and adultery and gluttony. But do you think he has only one strategy for using food and sex to bring about rebellion against the true God?

Whispers of the Fall

Compare his strategy in 1 Timothy 4 with his strategy in Genesis 3. His very first question to humankind was about food. It went like this: "Did God actually say, 'You shall not eat of any tree in the garden'?" (Gen. 3:1).

What had God said about eating from the trees of Eden? Genesis 2:16–17: "The LORD God commanded the man, saying, 'You may surely eat of *every* tree of the garden, but of the tree of the knowledge of good and evil you shall not eat, for in the day that you eat of it you shall surely die.'"

So what was God saying? He was saying: "I have given you life, and I have given you a world full of pleasures—pleasures of taste and sight and sound and smell and feel and nourishment. Only one tree is forbidden to you. And the point of that prohibition is to preserve the pleasures of this world. If you eat of that one, you will be saying to me: 'Your will is less authoritative than mine, your wisdom less wise than mine, your goodness less generous than mine, and your Fatherhood less caring than mine.' So don't eat from that tree. Keep on submitting to my will, and affirming my wisdom, and being thankful for my generosity, and trusting joyfully in my fatherly care. There are ten thousand trees with every imaginable fruit for pleasure and nourishment within a two-hour walk of where we stand. They are all good—very good—and they are all yours. Go, eat, enjoy, be thankful."

And what does Satan make of that? He made of it a tightfisted God. He took the prohibition of one suicidal tree and treated it as a prohibition of all: "Did God actually say, 'You shall not eat of *any* tree in the garden'?" (Gen. 3:1). Now, we could linger long here to see how this seed of distrust in God's generosity took root in Eve. But that's not the point here. The point is Satan's strategy and how it compares to 1 Timothy 4.

His strategy was to portray God as stingy, withholding something good of his creation from Adam and Eve. And in Genesis 3, Satan wanted Eve to believe that God is a withholder of good, and he wanted her to rebel. And that's what happened.

The Deceiver Uses Gluttony and Asceticism

Now, in 1 Timothy 4, Satan again wants us to see God as a withholder. For those who want to know him best, and rise to the level of the really spiritual, they should realize God prefers if they not experience sexual pleasures in marriage, and he prefers that they not experience the pleasurable sensations of certain foods. The demonic teaching is the same: God was a withholder in the garden, and he is still a withholder.

The difference is: in the garden, Satan wanted us to reject the God of the garden, and here in 1 Timothy 4, Satan wants us to embrace him. Either way, he accomplishes his purpose. The true God is not known or loved or trusted or treasured. If you reject God because you've been deceived, or embrace God because you've been deceived, the result is the same: you are wedded to a false god—a god of deception. And in the end, that's all Satan cares about. He couldn't care less if your false god taught gluttony or asceticism, free sex or celibacy. It makes no difference to him. He knows better than we do: this world of sight and sound and smell and touch and taste—this world and every pleasure in it—is designed for the worship of the true God. And if Satan can use abstinence or gluttony to promote a false, stingy God, he's fine with either strategy. All food is for the sake of knowing and enjoying the true God.

Paul's Response

On this, Satan and St. Paul are agreed. So let's turn to verses 3b–5 and see how Paul responds to this teaching of demons. Let's read verses 3–5 again:

> [The hypocritical advocates of the teaching of demons] forbid marriage and require abstinence from foods that God created to be received with thanksgiving by those who believe and know the truth. For everything created by God is good, and nothing is to be rejected if it is received with thanksgiving, for it is made holy [sanctified] by the word of God and prayer.

One way of describing Paul's response to the teaching of demons is to say: *Eating is not worship, but eating may become worship.* And verses 3–5 are Paul's explanation of how that happens—how eating and sexual relations become worship.

Not Worship—but Can Be

Sexual relations in marriage are not worship but may become worship. Smelling toast and bacon early in the morning is not worship but may become worship. Feeling fall breezes on the skin, and fall sunshine on the face, and fall colors in the eyes, and fall fragrances in the nose, are not worship, but they may become worship. Tasting and enjoying the pleasures of this world are not worshiping or honoring or loving or supremely treasuring God but may become that.

Millions of people worldwide are enjoying and being sustained by God's glorious creation today in some park or pasture or some gorgeous manifestation of his goodness in nature. And for some of them—I pray many—this enjoyment comes like a stab of longing that Lewis called "Joy" or "Romanticism." A stab of longing that whispers: "This beauty will not satisfy your soul; it beckons you toward something you do not yet know." That's how Lewis came to Christ. But first he had to learn: this joy, these stabs of longing, are not worship. But they can become worship.

Help from Lewis

Lewis devoted an entire chapter in his book *Miracles* to the fear he felt that in coming to Christ he would lose nature—lose the material world: "Where will you go to seek the wildness?" he asked.[2] And what he discovered was that only Christianity, with her doctrines of creation and the fall, portrayed and preserved nature as the horrible, wonderful, lovable, wild thing that she is.[3] He feared that if she were dethroned as the main thing, her lure to him, and his love to her, would be over. But instead he discovered this: "Because we love something else more than this world, we love even this world better than those who know no other."[4]

Or as he said in a letter to a woman who feared losing the memory of her husband,

When I have learnt to love God better than my earthly dearest, I shall love my earthly dearest better than I do now. In so far as I learn to love my earthly dearest at the expense of God and instead of God, I shall be moving towards the state in which I shall

---

[2] C. S. Lewis, *Miracles: A Preliminary Study* (New York: Macmillan, 1947), 65.
[3] "This attitude [a kind of asceticism that has a healthy respect for the very thing being rejected] will, I think, be found to depend logically on the doctrines of Creation and the Fall. Some hazy adumbrations of a doctrine of the Fall can be found in Paganism; but it is quite astonishing how rarely outside Christianity we find—I am not sure that we ever find—a real doctrine of Creation." C. S. Lewis, "Some Thoughts," in *Essay Collection and Other Short Pieces* (London: HarperCollins, 2000), 733.
[4] C. S. Lewis, "Some Thoughts," 734.

not love my earthly dearest at all. When first things are put first, second things are not suppressed but increased.[5]

Lewis certainly believed this about nature as well as people. If it is a first thing, we will not lose it. If it is second, it will be more wild and wonderful than ever. In the full flower of his Christian faith, while defending *super*naturalism with all his might, Lewis said, "She [Nature] has never seemed to me more great or more real than at this moment."[6]

In the chapter on charity in *The Four Loves*, he put it like this:

> Emerson has said, "When half-gods go, the gods arrive." That is a very doubtful maxim. Better say, "When God arrives (and only then) the half-gods can remain." Left to themselves they either vanish or become demons.[7]

God Created These

What Paul is doing in 1 Timothy 4:1–5 is showing how God arrives in the eating of food so that food can remain the glory that it is rather than vanishing or becoming a demon. Look with me at how Paul's argument flows here. I want you to see this for yourself. Verse 3: "They forbid marriage and require abstinence from foods"—and here starts Paul's response and argument—". . . foods that *God created* . . ." That's the first response. "These things you are rejecting are God's creation."

Paul will come back to this in verse 4 and draw out the implication of the goodness of creation, but here his point is that creation has a purpose. So he says in verse 3, ". . . that God created *to be received* [literally a prepositional phrase of purpose "for receiving, or for sharing in"] *with thanksgiving by those who believe and know the truth.*" So Paul's response is: "You hypocrites say these foods are to be renounced. God says, they are to be received. That's why they were created, to be received, shared in. That's their purpose."

[5] C. S. Lewis, *The Collected Letters of C. S. Lewis, vol. 3: Narnia, Cambridge, and Joy, 1950–1963,* ed. *Walter Hooper* (San Francisco: HarperSanFrancisco, 2007), 247.
[6] Lewis, *Miracles,* 65.
[7] C. S. Lewis, *The Four Loves* (London: Geoffrey Bles, 1960), 109.

For Those Who Believe

And food was not created to be received in *just any way* or by *just anybody*. There is a way food is to be received, and there is a kind of human for whom food was created to be received. Food was "created to be received *with thanksgiving*" (v. 3). Food was not created only to keep us alive or give us physical pleasure. Food was created by God in order that God might be thanked. Hence: eating is not worship, but it may become worship. Where there is no thankfulness to God in the heart, eating is not worship but a kind of prostitution. Eating minus gratefulness to God is not what eating was created to be.

And not only was food created by God to be received in a certain way; it also was created to be received by a certain group, namely, those who believe and those who know the truth. Verse 3: ". . . God created [food and sex] to be received with thanksgiving *by those who believe and know the truth*." The most obvious thing to point out is that now we see three acts that make eating what it is meant to be, and none of them is an act of the stomach or the taste buds. There is *thanking* and there is *believing* and there is *knowing*. So the most obvious thing to see is that at least part of what makes eating worship is acts that are not in themselves eating.

Eating food becomes worship by acts that terminate on God, not merely on food. Thanking is *for* food but *to* God. Believing is believing in *God* and his Son, Jesus Christ. Knowing terminates on *truth* and ultimately on *God*. Eating is not worship. Eating becomes worship—through knowing and believing and thanking. The created world is not an end in itself. It finds its meaning when people, created in God's image, use it with a mind that knows God and a heart that believes in and thanks God.

What Makes Eating Good

Paul's response to the ascetics continues in verse 4: "For everything created by God is good, and nothing is to be rejected if it is received with thanksgiving." Now Paul draws out the sweeping implication of God's creating food and sex: the implication is that they are good. "Everything created by God is good." It is the teaching of demons to imply that physical or material reality, in its created essence, is defective. And because of this Paul says in verse 4, "Nothing is to be rejected."

Well, no, not exactly. In fact, it is absolutely crucial that we realize this is not Paul's argument. Paul does not argue: "Creation is good, therefore nothing is to be rejected." He does not argue: "Creation is good, therefore eating is good." He does not argue: "Food is from God, and good and enjoyable, therefore eating is good and enjoyable and honors God." That's not what he says.

What he says is: "Everything created by God is good, and nothing is to be rejected *if it is received with thanksgiving.*" The divine goodness of food does not make eating food good. What makes eating good food good—or at least one essential part of what makes it good—is the thankfulness of our hearts. What makes the act of the mouth good is the act of the heart.

Sanctifying the Good Creation

Then finally Paul puts the final explanation in place for why thanking and believing and knowing are essential for the right uses of food and sex. Verse 5: "For [in this way] it [everything God has made, "nothing is to be rejected," v. 4] is made holy [sanctified] by the word of God and prayer."

The clearest and most important thing to see here is that the *good* creation must become the *sanctified* creation. It's not enough for creation to be *good* from God's side; it must be *sanctified* from our side. It won't do to say that because creation is good, eating is good. Eating may be fraud. Prostitution. In order for eating not to be fraudulent, the food must be sanctified. Not just good by creation but sanctified by the Word of God and prayer.

How Eating Becomes Holy

What does it mean for food to be "sanctified," or "made holy"? Last year I stood here at this conference and argued that *God's* holiness is his infinite worth owing to his transcendent, self-existent uniqueness. And *our* holiness is feeling and thinking and acting in accord with the infinite worth of God. And a *thing* becomes holy by being set apart for God as a means of expressing his infinite worth.

So, for example, Jesus said, "Which is greater, the gold or the temple that *has made the gold holy*?" (Matt. 23:17). Here the use of gold *in the temple* "sanctifies" the gold (same word "sanctifies" as in 1 Tim. 4:5). The gold is not itself changed, but it is given a God-exalting function by the way it is made part of God's temple. It is set apart for God as a means of expressing his infinite worth.

So sanctifying food, or making food holy, means setting it apart as a means of expressing the infinite worth of God. This is how eating becomes worship. This is how all things become pure. "To the pure, all things are pure" (Titus 1:15). Because the pure are the holy, and the holy sanctify all things by the Word of God and prayer.

By God's Speaking and Ours

How do the Word of God and prayer sanctify food? How do they set it apart as an expression of the infinite worth of God? The most obvious observation is that the *Word of God* is God's speaking to us, and *prayer* is our speaking to God.

So the general answer is that food is set apart as an expression of God's worth when we listen to what God has to say about food (and believe him, as v. 3 says), and when we speak back to him our affirmations of his truth with gratefulness and with believing pleas that he help us taste his worth in this way.

"Nothing to Give but Himself"

Now, to make the answer more specific, we could go so many different directions at this point. Because God has told us so many things in his Word about how food relates to him.[8] But I am going to focus on just one thing suggested by C. S. Lewis in a provocative section in *Letters to Malcolm: Chiefly on Prayer*. Here's the excerpt:

> Creation seems to be delegation through and through. He will do nothing simply of Himself which can be done by creatures. I suppose this is because He is a giver. And He has nothing to give but Himself. And to give Himself is to do His deeds—in a sense, and on varying levels to be Himself—through the things He has made.
>
> In Pantheism God is all. But the whole point of creation surely is that He was not content to be all. He intends to be "all *in all*."[9]

I am sure I do not understand all Lewis means by this. But it seems to me that he is onto something that has profound implications for the way food is sanctified in our use of it. He says, "He has nothing to give but Himself." Now that strikes me as true before creation.

Before creation, when God contemplated creating beings who would experience maximum joy with him forever, he had no treasure chest outside himself to look into and ponder which of these would make his creatures happy. He was the treasure. He alone existed. He alone was of infinite value. So when he created the material universe for us to live in—food, sex, colors, sounds, tastes, textures—he was doing it to give us himself for our enjoyment.

He was not saying: "I am not enough for you; so I will supplement the gift of myself with the gift of physical things, since the gift of myself would be less satisfying than the gift of me plus physical things." That's not why he made the world. There's another possibility. And that's what Lewis is getting at.

---

[8] E.g., he has told us that he created it; that it is good (1 Tim. 4:4); that it not only is meant to sustain life but to give pleasure (1 Tim. 6:17); that food like all other creation exists for the glory of God (Ps. 19:1; 1 Cor. 10:31; Col. 1:16); and that we are sinners and do not deserve any of this goodness (Rom. 1:18; 3:9), so that for believers food is an absolutely free foretaste of glory bought with the blood of Christ (Rom. 8:32).

[9] C. S. Lewis, *Letters to Malcolm, Chiefly on Prayer* (San Diego: Harcourt, 1963), 71 (emphasis original).

Why God Made the World

As God contemplates creating the world, Lewis says, "He has nothing to give but Himself. And to give Himself is to do His deeds—in a sense, and on varying levels to be Himself—through the things He has made." In other words, God creates the physical world for man to live in so that in and through the vast diversities of goodness in creation, God could communicate his own vast diversities of goodness to us.

Which means that the physical universe is thus not an added treasure alongside God. Rather, the universe is the kind of garden or orchard where human beings can best taste and see the manifold goodness of God himself.

I'm suggesting, along with Lewis, that of all the possible ways that God could have revealed the fullness and diversity of the supreme value of his being, he concluded that a physical world would be the best. The material creation was not God's way of saying to humankind: "I am not enough for you." It was his way of saying: "Here is the best garden where more of what I am can be revealed to finite creatures. The juiciness of a peach and the sweetness of honey are a communication of myself."

In Jesus's Name

Remember Lewis's words: "He has nothing to give but Himself. And to give Himself is . . . to *be* Himself—through the things He has made." This is risky because it could be taken to mean pantheism—that the enjoyment of the peach and the honey is the enjoyment of God, because the peach and the honey are God. He could be taken that way.

But he tells us explicitly in the context *not* to take him that way. What Lewis wants to say is that to enjoy the juiciness of a peach and to enjoy the sweetness of honey is to enjoy God, not because the peach *is* God, or the honey *is* God, but because that kind of sweetness and pleasantness is indeed in God and from God, and this is the best way God can communicate his sweetness to us.

If Lewis is on the right track here, what then does 1 Timothy 4:5 mean when it says food "is made holy [or sanctified] by the word of God and prayer"? It means the Word of God teaches us to taste food as a communication of his diverse goodness and his supreme worth. And when we taste food as a communication of God's goodness and worth in the eating of this food, we offer up our prayers of thanks, and ask him to give us the fullest possible feast of his supreme worth. And we pray this in Jesus's name, knowing that every lasting blessing was bought by his blood.

Taste and See

Circling back to the beginning, it may be more obvious now why demons would promote teachings that communicate the defectiveness or inferiority of food and sex by forbidding them from the truly godly. This is, in the end, a demonic attack on the holiness of God— on the supreme worth and excellence of God.

And Paul's response to it is: rejecting food is not the path of holiness. Sanctifying food is the path of holiness. God made it. It's good. But that goodness does not make eating worship. The Word of God and prayer make food holy and make eating worship. And they do it by showing us how to taste the sweetness of God in the sweetness of honey and give him thanks.

May God take all the messages of this book, and all the wisdom of C. S. Lewis, and all the wonders of this world, and all the truth of his Word, and grant you to taste and see that the Lord is good. And with the help of C. S. Lewis may you communicate it with a joy and skill as never before to a world full of unsatisfied longing.

APPENDIX I

C. S. Lewis and the Doctrine of Hell

RANDY ALCORN

> The safest road to hell is the gradual one—the gentle slope, soft underfoot, without sudden turnings, without milestones, without signposts.
>
> C. S. Lewis, *The Screwtape Letters*

Lewis said many profound and fascinating things about hell. Some are biblically precise, while others are more abstract and subject to misunderstanding. In some cases, his views are not solidly biblical. But many of his insights on hell are true to Scripture, and some of his speculations are compelling food for thought.

Hell: Grave Injustice or Ultimate Justice?

Lewis said in *The Great Divorce*, "There are only two kinds of people in the end: those who say to God, 'Thy will be done,' and those to whom God says, in the end, 'Thy will be done.'"[1]

Of course, God does not fully let people have their way, since it is clear, for instance, that the rich man in Luke 16 wants out of hell but cannot escape it. Lewis's point is, when someone says, "I do not want to have a relationship with God," in that limited sense they ultimately get their way. The unbeliever's "wish" to be away from God turns out to be his worst nightmare.

Nonetheless, those who do not want God *do* want goodness and

---

[1] C. S. Lewis, *The Great Divorce* (New York: Collier, 1946), 72.

happiness. But what makes anything good is God. Second Thessalonians 1:9 describes hell like this: "They will suffer the punishment of eternal destruction, away from the presence of the Lord." Where God withdraws, there can be no good. So, in Lewis's terms, the unbeliever gets what he wants—God's absence—yet with it gets what he doesn't want—the loss of all good.

C. S. Lewis said of hell, "There is no doctrine which I would more willingly remove from Christianity than this, if it lay in my power. But it has the full support of Scripture and, specially, of our Lord's own words; it has always been held by Christendom; and it has the support of reason."[2]

Most of what Lewis says here is solidly biblical. Where there may be a chink in his logic is exactly where it is for many of us. We wish there were no hell—and imagine this comes from our sense of goodness and kindness. But God *could* remove hell yet chooses not to. Do we have more confidence in our goodness than his?

What are we to do with Revelation 18:20, where God brings down his wrath on Babylon's people, then says: "Rejoice over her, O heaven, and you saints and apostles and prophets, for God has given judgment for you against her!"? Doesn't this suggest that in heaven we will see sin's horrors clearly and have far stronger convictions about hell's justice?

Hell is not pleasant, appealing, or encouraging. But neither is it evil; rather, it's a place where evil is judged. Indeed, if being sentenced to hell is just punishment, then the absence of hell would itself be evil.

Hell Itself Is Morally Good, Because a Good God Must Punish Evil

Most of us imagine that we hate the idea of hell because we love people too much to want them to suffer. But that implies God loves them less. Our revulsion is understandable, but what about hell makes us cringe? Is it the wickedness that's being punished? Is it the

---

[2] C. S. Lewis, *The Problem of Pain* (New York: Macmillan, 1962), 118.

suffering of those who might have turned to Christ? Or do we cringe because we imagine hell's punishments are wicked or disproportionate? These very different responses expose different views of God.

Perhaps we hate hell too much because we don't hate evil enough. This is something that could have been developed more in Lewis's thinking. The same could be said of many of us.

If we regard hell as a divine overreaction to sin, we deny that God has the moral right to inflict ongoing punishment on any humans. By denying hell, we deny the extent of God's holiness. When we minimize sin's seriousness, we minimize God's grace in Christ's blood, shed for us. For if the evils he died for aren't significant enough to warrant eternal punishment, perhaps the grace displayed on the cross isn't significant enough to warrant eternal praise.

How Jesus Viewed Hell

In the Bible, Jesus spoke more about hell than anyone else did. He referred to hell as a real place (see Matt. 10:28; 13:40–42; Mark 9:43–48). He described it in graphic terms: a fire that burns but doesn't consume, an undying worm that eats away at the damned, and a lonely, foreboding darkness.

Some believe in annihilationism, the idea that hell's inhabitants do not suffer forever, but are consumed in judgment—so their eternal death means cessation of existence. Edward Fudge, in his book and DVD *The Fire That Consumes*, defends this position, one that John Stott also embraced. It's an argument I have considered seriously, one that holds up to much of the Old Testament revelation, but which I find very difficult to reconcile with Jesus's words: "And these will go away into eternal punishment, but the righteous into eternal life" (Matt. 25:46). Or with the words of Revelation 20:10, which speak of not only Satan but two human beings, the Antichrist and the false prophet, being cast into the lake of fire and "tormented day and night forever and ever." Revelation 14:11 appears to apply to a large number of people: "And the smoke of their torment goes up forever and ever."

Christ says the unsaved "will be thrown into the outer darkness. In that place there will be weeping and gnashing of teeth" (Matt. 8:12). He taught that an unbridgeable chasm separates the wicked in hell from the righteous in Paradise. The wicked suffer terribly, remain conscious, retain their memories, long for relief, cannot find comfort, cannot leave their torment, and have no hope (see Luke 16:19–31). In short, our Savior could not have painted a bleaker picture of hell. It is one that C. S. Lewis, with reluctance, believed and affirmed, bowing his knee in submission to a higher authority.

Lewis said, "I have met no people who fully disbelieved in hell and also had a living and life-giving belief in Heaven."[3] The biblical teaching on both destinations stands or falls together. When heaven and hell are spoken of in Scripture, each place is portrayed as being just as real and, in some passages anyway, as permanent as the other.

Lewis's friend, Dorothy Sayers, said it well:

> There seems to be a kind of conspiracy to forget, or to conceal, where the doctrine of hell comes from. The doctrine of hell is not "mediaeval priestcraft" for frightening people into giving money to the church: it is Christ's deliberate judgment on sin. . . . We cannot repudiate hell without altogether repudiating Christ.[4]

The Problem of Emeth in *The Last Battle*

Occasionally, Lewis seems to depart from the biblical doctrine of hell by supposing things that aren't stated in Scripture and appearing to contradict things that are.

In *The Last Battle*, the soldier Emeth, who served the demon Tash, is welcomed into heaven though he did not serve Aslan, the Christ figure, by name. Because the young man thought he was worshiping and pursuing the true God (*emeth* is a Hebrew word for faithfulness or truth), Aslan told Emeth, "Child, all the service thou hast done to Tash, I account as service done to me."

---

[3] C. S. Lewis, *Letters to Malcolm: Chiefly on Prayer* (Boston: Houghton Mifflin Harcourt, 2002), 76.
[4] Dorothy Sayers, *Introductory Papers on Dante* (London: Methuen, 1954), 44.

Some have used this passage to charge Lewis with being a universalist, though Lewis's other writings clearly show he was not. But this passage does imply Lewis believed in a kind of inclusivism, where in some cases, mentally responsible people who have not embraced Christ in this life may ultimately be saved. The criterion for salvation, then, is not believing in Jesus while still here (John 1:12; 14:6; Acts 4:12; Rom. 10:9–10). Rather, in some cases, God may consider it sufficient that someone has followed a false god with true motives.

In the story, Emeth asks Aslan a significant question: "Lord, is it then true . . . that thou and Tash are one?" Aslan's response leaves no room for confusion:

> The Lion growled so that the earth shook and said, "It is false. Not because he and I are one, but because we are opposites.
>
> "For I and he are of such different kinds that no service which is vile can be done to me, and none which is not vile can be done to him. Therefore, if any man swear by Tash and keep his oath for the oath's sake, it is by me that he has truly sworn, and it is I who reward him. And if any man do a cruelty in my name, then it is Tash whom he serves and by Tash his deed is accepted. . . ."
>
> "Beloved," said the Glorious One, "unless thy desire had been for me thou wouldst not have sought so long and so truly. For all find what they truly seek."[5]

Aslan categorically affirms he and Tash are in no sense alike. Indeed, Aslan despises the demon! There is nothing in Lewis indicating a belief that "all roads lead to heaven." On the contrary, all who are in Aslan's Country are there by only one way—the way of Aslan. Emeth is saved by Aslan—no one and nothing else. Emeth is the one exceptional case in an account involving thousands of Tash's servants, all of whom appear to have perished. Emeth seems to be Lewis's one hopeful exception, certainly not the rule.

---

[5] C. S. Lewis, *The Last Battle* (New York: Collier, 1956), 164–65.

Emeth's Better Parallel: Cornelius

The Bible clearly states that "it is appointed for man to die once, and after that comes judgment" (Heb. 9:27). There are accounts in Scripture of people continuing to exist after they die (e.g., Luke 16:19–31) but no account of someone making a decision to turn to Christ after death.

Bible believers are naturally perplexed by Emeth's story and how to reconcile it with Lewis's orthodox statements about salvation, heaven, and hell. But we should certainly welcome the *biblical* kind of inclusivism that offers the gospel to everyone, and rejoices that people of every tribe, nation, and language will worship God together forever (Rev. 5:9–10; 7:9). We should celebrate stories like that of Cornelius, whose service God accepted even before drawing him to a full understanding of the gospel (Acts 10:2, 22, 31).

Emeth's story would have paralleled Cornelius's if Aslan had come to the young man *before* his death. That would have been my preference, certainly. But even with occasional imperfections, of which Emeth may be most prominent, the great truths of the Chronicles of Narnia remain clear, strong, and biblically resonant. So do the remarkable insights about heaven and the new earth in Lewis's writings that I deal with in chapter 5 and the other Christ-honoring insights of Lewis that fill this book.

(People sometimes ask me why I tolerate Lewis's more troubling doctrine. My answer is that his trajectory is toward the gospel, not away from it, and that God has used him to speak into my life Christ-centered and paradigm-shifting biblical truths. I do not have to embrace 100 percent of what Lewis said to benefit from that 85 percent that is so incredibly rich.)

Because Our Choices in This Life Shape Us Forever, God Rejecters Might Be as Miserable in Heaven as in Hell

In *The Problem of Pain*, C. S. Lewis spoke to those who argue against the doctrine of hell:

In the long run the answer to all those who object to the doctrine of hell is itself a question: "What are you asking God to do?" To wipe out their past sins and, at all costs, to give them a fresh start, smoothing every difficulty and offering every miraculous help? But He has done so, on Calvary. To forgive them? They will not be forgiven. To leave them alone? Alas, I am afraid that is what He does.[6]

He adds this oft-quoted statement: "The damned are, in one sense, successful, rebels to the end; the doors of hell are locked on the inside. . . . They enjoy forever the horrible freedom they have demanded, and are therefore self-enslaved."[7]

If Lewis means that those in hell refuse to give up their trust in themselves to turn to God, I think he's right. While they long to escape from hell, that is not the same as longing to be with God and repenting.

Lewis speaks in *The Great Divorce* of "the demand of the loveless and the self-imprisoned that they should be allowed to blackmail the universe: that till they consent to be happy (on their own terms) no one else shall taste joy: that theirs should be the final power; that hell should be able to veto heaven."[8]

Heaven and hell are places defined, respectively, by God's presence or absence, by God's grace or wrath. Whose we are, not where we are, determines our misery or our joy. To transport a man from hell to heaven would bring him no joy unless he had a transformed relationship with God, a regenerating work that can be done only by the Holy Spirit (John 1:12–13; 3:3–8; Rom. 6:14; 1 Cor. 2:12, 14).

To the person sealed forever in righteousness, God will remain wondrous; to the one sealed forever in sin, God will remain dreadful. If we reject the best gift that a holy and gracious God can offer us, purchased with his blood, what remains, in the end, will be nothing but hell.

---

[6] Lewis, *The Problem of Pain*, 128.
[7] Ibid.
[8] Lewis, *The Great Divorce*, 120 (emphasis original).

Lewis also said in *The Great Divorce*, "All that are in hell, choose it. Without that self-choice there could be no hell. No soul that seriously and constantly desires joy will ever miss it. Those who seek find. To those who knock it is opened."

This too is insightful but can be taken too far. One can desire joy outside of God and not find it, of course, but I take it that Lewis speaks of one who earnestly seeks the true God, the source of all joy. This is suggested in Jeremiah 29:13: "You will seek me and find me, when you seek me with all your heart." And in Matthew 7:7, "Ask, and it will be given to you; seek, and you will find; knock, and it will be opened to you."

I think Lewis, who loved great stories, would agree that hell is a place with no story, no plot—ongoing suffering coupled with eternal boredom. Ironically, Satan labors to portray heaven, from which he was cast out, as boring and undesirable. The Bible, on the other hand, portrays the new heavens and the new earth as the setting for joy without end. If we think correctly about heaven, we will realize that because God is infinitely great and gracious, heaven is the ultimate adventure while hell is the ultimate sinkhole.

Perhaps the best last word to give Lewis is this: "To enter heaven is to become more human than you ever succeeded in being on earth; to enter hell is to be banished from humanity."[9]

---

[9] Lewis, *The Problem of Pain*, 124.

APPENDIX 2

A Conversation with the Contributors, September 28, 2013

RANDY ALCORN, JOHN PIPER, PHILIP RYKEN, KEVIN VANHOOZER, DOUGLAS WILSON, AND DAVID MATHIS

The following is a lightly edited transcript of the panel discussion held on September 28, 2013, at the Desiring God National Conference, where the chapters of this book were originally delivered as conference plenaries. David Mathis's questions are in italics.

Let's begin with some of our disagreements and places of tempered enthusiasm with C. S. Lewis. Phil and Randy already have noted his doctrines of Scripture and hell. Doug talked about some seeming inconsistencies in his soteriology. Any other theological concerns with Lewis worth noting here?

Douglas Wilson: Lewis was an Anglican who had no problem with the system of bishops and that sort of thing. So as Baptists and Presbyterians I think that we would say, all rightly, that we are not enthusiastic about bishops. But Lewis in another place acknowledges that Puritans were not the dour types. He says, "Bishops, not beer, were their chief aversion." But he didn't have a problem with that. So we don't belong to the Church of England like he did, and he was a faithful churchman in that communion. I think that it's a Christian communion, but I think that this issue would be a notable difference (more so back then than it is now), but that doesn't go to the heart of anything significant.

So given the disagreements mentioned here and throughout the confer-
ence, why love Lewis? Why commend Lewis? Why speak at a conference
on Lewis? What is it about Lewis that you would want to commend others
to read?

John Piper: The way I had thought of the question is, "Why, John
Piper, do you not only read him and like him and benefit from him
but also have a conference on him? You wouldn't do that with certain
living people who believed what he believed." That's a true statement. So either I'm inconsistent or there's something else going on.
And it's the other things that are going on that we were talking about.
I'll just mention one, and then these guys can be thinking about what
the others are.

Lewis, unlike so many of the people whom I stumble over today,
epistemologically was a realist, an objectivist. He loved objective
truth. He believed in reason. He loved propositional truth. He was
lucid. There was no spin in Lewis. There was no fuzz and no froth
and no obfuscation. So that is a piece. I can go a long way with a person who may disagree with me on certain points if we're both totally
into what the Bible says is true and who believes that you can know
it. And you are not trying to massage or conceal or soften the truth. So
that's one reason I'm just drawn to him and find so much help in him.

Philip Ryken: I think it's a good reminder for even the theologians
that we feel most affinity to. There are always some places of warning
or imbalance. No one apart from our Lord himself is a perfect theologian. So I think reading C. S. Lewis reminds us of that. I would also
say there are a lot of personal reasons for appreciating C. S. Lewis,
and I can't probably say with Doug that what I've learned from Lewis
outweighs what I've learned from everybody else, but I will say no
one has had a bigger impact on my Christian experience than C. S.
Lewis. A lot of it was formative from childhood—what you learn
about courage and what it means to live a life of faithfulness, even
from the Narnian Chronicles. So, when you have an author who has

that large of a life-shaping influence, you recognize the value and benefit of that writer.

Also just to say briefly that I think one thing that distinguishes Lewis from some of the people you may have in mind—living authors that you wouldn't commend in a conference setting like this—is that Lewis is very clear that he wants to be in submission to the authority of Scripture. There are some people in the church today who you sometimes get the sense are standing a little bit in authority over Scripture and who have their own opinions. They sometimes think they know a little better than the Bible. You don't get that sense from C. S. Lewis. He wants to be orthodox and in submission to God's authority.

Randy Alcorn: I think, too, a lot of Christian leaders today are drifting, and they've grown up holding to truths that they are now departing from. Their trajectory is away from the gospel. Lewis came from atheism, moving to theism, then agnosticism, and then he came to a life-changing faith in Christ. He was growing in his life as he came from a world where he didn't have the doctrinal reference points. And even though it's not an excuse, his trajectory was always, in my opinion, toward the gospel—if not always, it was usually toward the gospel from the outside. Also, consider the fact that he did not profess to be a professional theologian. He just made that clear. Now, of course, when you're a person of influence you would wish that you would do more study in these different areas. But to me it's so different because here's a living, vibrant faith of someone who came from the outside. And for me as a young believer I soaked it up because I remember when I didn't know God—like it was just three months ago. I didn't know God, and he didn't know God, and he came to know God, and he's really smart. I can follow his line of reasoning. And my faith makes sense, and I can defend that faith. So to me, C. S. Lewis was a godsend, and his doctrinal weaknesses are real, but they're not debilitating. And we should read him selectively as we should read everyone else selectively. Be like the Bereans, who were more noble than the Thessalonicans and searched the Scriptures daily to see whether these things are true (Acts 17:11).

Kevin Vanhoozer: I agree that the substance of Lewis is soundly orthodox, which is why I trust him. But I want to mention two other factors that appeal to me in particular. First, the quality of his writing. He has set the bar over which I keep stumbling. The work of the theologian and the preacher is, to a large extent, a ministry of the word. It's word-craft. And Lewis was a master of the craft.

The second item I can think of is that he was a student of the classics. So he was less prone to be influenced by the prevailing winds of cultural fashion. He read old books. And he could see trends come and go, and some trends do come and go in different cultural guises. I think one thing that particularly impressed me was how he might have had his finger up and sensed the winds of postmodernity before it actually arrived. I'm thinking of an essay. It isn't often discussed, but I really like it. It's the one called "Bulverism." I don't think anybody's used that term yet. But that essay tells a story.

Randy Alcorn: I was going to use that tonight, but I'm just going to leave it out.

Philip Ryken: Can you describe "Bulverism" for us?

Kevin Vanhoozer: It's the name of a person in his little article. He imagines a boy. It was Eugene or Edward, something with an *E*, I think. And his last name is Bulver. And the little boy is listening to his parents argue, and at one point his mother says to his father, "Oh, you say that because you're a man." And for Bulver, a little light goes off, and he realizes, "I don't have to answer the objection. I just have to point out where the person is coming from. Don't deal with the arguments. Just identify their location." That is exactly what I see many postmoderns doing. They simply say reason is situated. It comes from here. You say that because you're a conservative or because you're a theist or because you're a fill-in-the-blank. And then you don't have to deal with the argument. You simply locate where it comes from. And Lewis actually had a name for it—*Bulverism*. Of course it doesn't work if I meet a postmodernist. I can't say, "You're a Bulverist," because no one knows what that is. But that impresses me about Lewis.

Douglas Wilson: If I could say what I appreciated—this will be a combination of what John and Kevin said. If we laid out all the areas where we agree and disagree with Lewis on an atemporal grid, we could add up the percentages and say that we agree this much or whatever. But if you look at the twentieth century and ask what the *central* error was, what's the central heresy of our time? I think that relativism, subjectivism, me-ism is *the* central error of our time. And Lewis didn't give an inch when it came to that sort of thing. He was virtually the only one standing in the gap, fighting that particular battle. And I'll take it. I love that man because he's *contra mundum*. He's against the world. At a particular time when all of the world is going one way, he's not going there. The places where I think I disagree with him, I'm reassured because—going back to the doctrine of Scripture—he doesn't say something like, "There are mistakes in Scripture because there are miracles, and, of course, miracles don't happen." His reasoning is completely in another direction—I think wrong, but he's not being blown by the spirit of the age. He called himself "an old Western man," a dinosaur. And that's what we needed at that point in time.

So personally in what ways has Lewis shaped you in who you are now? Particular insights? Concepts? Particular places where he says things? How have you been shaped by him?

John Piper: Chronological snobbery came along as a reality he alerted me to in my twenties, which said that something is not truer because it's newer but that the old may be more beautiful and more true. So don't ever equate new with better. That puts you out of step with your century very quickly. Which is a wonderful place to be. There's a freedom in being a dinosaur in the twentieth and twenty-first centuries. That was a huge one for me. Love old things. Assess things by virtue of absolute and eternal standards, not by how trendy and cool they are.

The second one for me was what Alan Jacobs calls an "omnivorous attentiveness." That means Lewis saw things. And I think that's part of what you're getting at, Kevin. Lewis has such great eyes. He saw things. And Clyde Kilby, who embodied him for me, saw the world in a similar way. He saw trees, and he saw toads. He refers to toads a lot. And he taught me that nothing interesting can be said about toads. The only thing that can be said is that this toad has bulging eyes and bumps on his back and bumps a funny way when he jumps.

In other words, he helped me escape from the dangers of abstraction and move toward concreteness. And when I've taught preaching with some of the guys that are out there, I'm just pleading continually toward concreteness, which is almost the same as what we've been saying about likening or metaphor, but it's not the same. To move from a tree to an oak and from an oak to the white oak and from the white oak to the one in the front yard and from the one in the front yard to the one where you carved your initials when you were engaged to your wife—it moves down to a kind of reality that's engaging and palpable and moving to people. And so those two things are what I learned from Lewis—chronological snobbery and being omnivorously attentive to concreteness.

Randy Alcorn: For me as a brand-new Christian—a teenager reading Lewis—the main lesson I learned was probably the love of God and the fear of God coming together in one person, Aslan, Lewis's portrayal of Jesus Christ, where you see Mr. Beaver respond to one of the children's questions, "Is the lion safe?" Mr. Beaver answers, "Safe? No, he's not safe, but he's good." And then we love how Mr. Beaver states that Aslan is not a tame lion. We love the appropriate fear the children felt when they heard his roar. There was this response to his might and then the tenderness and the love and the great romp, and the children—Lucy in particular—grabbing onto his mane. I could see loving this God—and his love for me—and yet simultaneously I saw my need to never interpret his goodness as meaning he was tame, as if I could get him to do what I wanted him to do. It was really all about him and not about me, and yet he truly did love me. That was just formative to a huge degree for me.

Douglas Wilson: My folks read the Narnia stories to me. It started when I was five, and the books were still coming out, I think, in 1958. It was just all new and fresh. And I remember, for example, in *Prince Caspian* when Trumpkin doesn't believe in Aslan, but he's fighting on the good guys' side. And he doesn't believe in the horn, but they're just debating whether to blow the horn, and so they finally decide to do it. And then Dr. Cornelius says, "Well, we'll have to send two messengers out to different places where the help might come." And Trumpkin says, "I knew it. The first result of this tomfoolery is we're going to lose two fighters and not get help." Then someone does some backchat, and then Trumpkin volunteers to be one of the people to go. And someone says, "But, Trumpkin, I thought you didn't believe in the horn." And he says, "No more I do, your majesty. But I know the difference between giving advice and taking orders. You've had my advice. Now's the time for orders." Exactly! I've given you my input. And I learned authority from that.

So Lewis was a man under authority. It goes back to what I said earlier about him rejecting the subjectivist goo. He was a man under authority. But then it's not blind authority. It's not, "Wind me up and point me in the right direction," because Trumpkin goes on a mission he doesn't believe in just because he knows the difference between giving advice and taking orders. Someone suggests, "Well, why don't we bring in some ogres and hags and everybody?" And someone says, "Well, if we did that we wouldn't have Aslan on our side." And Trumpkin says, "What matters more is that you wouldn't have *me* on your side. All right? You bring in the ogres and hags, I'm gone." But if there's a policy disagreement in the boardroom, we take the vote and then I am all in. I'm going to take orders and I'm all in. I'm going to pursue that.

That's the way story shapes someone's whole outlook. Trumpkin comes up in my thoughts in long board meetings when it doesn't look like the vote's going to go the right way. Ugh. Okay. Be a Trumpkin.

Philip Ryken: That's exactly the kind of thing I'm talking about. I remember a time when a group of people thought they were acting in the interest of our group, but it would involve a lack of integrity that I was not willing to go along with. Even as they started to make the argument to me, I was able to say, "You know who I am. You know that there's nothing you can say that will convince me otherwise." I think that kind of character for me came from going through the wardrobe with Lucy and from being on the decks of the *Dawn Treader* with Reepicheep. It just shapes your life and character, and that's one of the reasons why it's so great to read the Narnia Chronicles to children. It shapes their lives.

Kevin Vanhoozer: I can think of four ways Lewis has influenced me as a reader.

Randy Alcorn: Is the first one Bulverism? No?

Kevin Vanhoozer: The first one was a humbling experience where he says you really aren't a reader if you only read a book once and leave it at that. And that was an "aha" moment for me. Second, he encouraged me to read an old book or maybe more than one old book for every new book I read. Third, he said you have to get the genre of a text right. You have to know what kind of a text you're reading. This is true of everything. Are you dealing with a corkscrew, he asks, or a cathedral? The question of genre, right identification of the kind of thing we're reading, comes first. I've made mistakes in genre. When I first read Jane Austen, I thought it was a serious story. I didn't catch the social satire in *Pride and Prejudice*. That's awful. It's a good thing

I read that book twice. But the most important way in which Lewis has influenced me—and again this is a book we haven't yet talked about—is his *An Experiment in Criticism*. He distinguishes using a book from interpreting or receiving it. We use books when we subject them to our will. We have the will to power as interpreters, and we make them say and do what we will. Receiving a text is quite different. One has to be spiritually humble. One has to be open to the proposal being made. It reminded me that reading itself can be an exercise in sanctification. Am I going to open myself up in all humility and receive the Word rather than twist it for my own purposes?

On that note, are there any obscure pieces Lewis wrote, like essays or his various letters, that you'd want to mention here? Is there perhaps something you have found to be gold in Lewis but don't hear commended often and would like to share?

Douglas Wilson: Two things, one more obscure than the other. He did an essay or a little booklet called *The Literary Impact of the Authorized Version*. He's just discussing the impact of the King James Version of the Bible. It's obscure, delightful. It's just very good. Less obscure but one I would commend is *A Preface to Paradise Lost*, which is not one of the top sellers, but there is some gold in that one.

Kevin Vanhoozer: As a theologian I have to mention, because you mention his *Preface to Paradise Lost*, his preface to Athanasius's treatise *On the Incarnation*. This was Lewis's introduction to a most important theologian, someone who was instrumental in carving out the doctrine of the Trinity in the fourth century, but he was particularly commenting on why it's important to get into the meat and potatoes of the doctrine of the incarnation and to let Athanasius do it.

There's another one in an essay called "Transposition" where you ask something obscure. I'm not sure I have a good grasp of what he is talking about, but it has to do with how lower things can be taken up into a higher medium and somehow become themselves, yet they remain themselves and yet they're transfigured in some way. Owen

Barfield thought that "Transposition" might be the closest thing Lewis had to a theory of the imaginations. I'm still mulling that over.

Philip Ryken: I would just really appeal to people. Even if you've read ten things by C. S. Lewis, there are probably at least ten more that would be an absolute delight for you. It's worth taking a little effort to find what some of those pieces are. I mean it's all great stuff. It really is—all of it. There are probably a few people at the conference who have read everything by Lewis. I certainly haven't read everything by Lewis. Even being here for these days has inspired me to go back and pull some things off the shelf and track down some things that I should read.

Randy Alcorn: One thing that comes to mind for me is *Letters to an American Lady*, which is not often quoted from, but the discipline of writing has been mentioned. This was something that was a huge burden for Lewis, and it was a service that he believed God had called him to do. And it required great sacrifice on his part. One time he wrote to this American lady, "Could you please not write to me on the holidays? I receive many more letters around Easter and Christmas, and it takes away some of the joy of the holidays." So you get that feel for it. Then he goes right on to answer in detail her letter. I remember one in particular that was only five months before Lewis died where the American lady, whose name in real life was Mary, was writing and talking about her fear of death and that maybe she was dying. And then he writes back to her: "Your sins are confessed. Has this world been so kind to you that you really feel you must stay?" Then he says, "Entrust yourself to God." Relax. Give yourself over to him. Then he says, "And this might not really be the time for your death." And then he says, "But make it a good rehearsal. Prepare for the day when it really will be your time." Then he signs off with something like, "Your fellow traveler who is also tired and ready to leave this world, Jack."

There are many other valuable little nuggets in his letters, certainly his letters to children. I do not respond personally to every letter from an adult, but I've made a policy that I will always respond to children. Lewis has been a huge example for me in that area, although he did much more of it and was much more sacrificial, because of the influence on a single person. I praise God for all those letters he wrote that we can benefit from now. So if you have not read his letters, please, please do. They're very rich.

Philip Ryken: Now I know how to get Randy to respond to my correspondence. I'll just put, "I'm an eight-year-old college president."

You mention the letters, and it called to mind another obscure book of C. S. Lewis's, *The Latin Letters of C. S. Lewis,* a correspondence in Latin to a Roman Catholic priest in Italy, I believe. It's in that book, I think, that he talks about his practice of praying for the lost. Lewis is writing to somebody who's kind of discouraged, not really seeing God at work in the world (in his opinion). And he agrees with that. So he says something along the lines of, "Sometimes you wonder what God is really doing. But I have a list in my journal of people I pray for who do not know Christ, and I have a list of people for whom I give thanks because they have come to Christ. The transference of people from one list to another is encouraging as I see God answering prayer over time." I wonder if people know about that aspect of Lewis's prayer life. Those are the kinds of gems you can find in some of these other writings.

John Piper: I want to address people who may not be book readers—they don't read books because they're too long and they just don't have the time. I think Lewis has dozens and dozens of two- to ten-page essays, and they're all worth reading. You can find them in *God in the Dock* and *Christian Reflections.* I've got an eight-hundred-page book that's not in print anymore, if you could find it, called *Essay Collection and Other Short Pieces.* Just some night sit on a chair, take a half hour to read a short piece, and it will be gold for you, almost any of them.

Randy Alcorn: One of those pieces, "Life on Other Planets," is very interesting reading. I mean, it's something that appeals. The breadth of what he wrote these short essays on is amazing.

John Piper: Yeah. There's even one called "Bicycles."

Let's talk about joviality. Doug, I think many of us are excited for the jovial Calvinistic vision at the end of your chapter. Describe the forms that jovial Calvinism takes in this world of pain and suffering.

Douglas Wilson: I guess the first thing I would say is that you have to be careful that the joviality is not sort of a Dr. Pangloss, like out of *Candide*, where someone who's going through a terrible world of suffering is not clued in to what's happening. That's not joviality. That's not someone who is responding appropriately. He needs to be dialed in. True joviality, I think, has to be understood as an act of defiance. The world is a mess. It is fallen. It's filled with wickedness. In *The Lion, the Witch and the Wardrobe* the White Witch comes across the feast in the woods and asks, "Why all this gluttony? Why all this self-indulgence?" Lewis captures that wonderfully. Judas is the one who wants to know why the ointment was not sold and given to the poor. Judas is the one who is being the skinflint. Judas was the one pinching the pennies—and there was a reason for that, as John tells us. The White Witch captures that wonderfully. If you're celebrating at some Sabbath dinner, or you're celebrating because you've never heard of any of the conflict, then you just are not clued in. But if you are at Rivendell, The Last Homely House—if you're feasting—then it's an act of defiance. It's a declaration of war. It's the recognition that this is how we fight. We are the cheerful warriors, the happy warriors, the cavalier. We should fight like a cavalier. We should fight like Dartanian and not like a thug. Right? We need to fight. We must fight, but the person who fights like a cavalier is an attractive leader. He's going to attract more people to his side. He's going to be more effective.

Think about a pro-life activist who says, "But they're killing babies, and it's terrible. And the whole world's falling apart. The whole world's going to hell." So they write their letter to the editor with a fisted crayon—what I like to call the *spittle-flecked letter*. That is, they can't say, "But abortion's so important, I've got to do it this way." I would say no. Abortion is so important that you must *not* do it that way. You're not venting; you're fighting. And if you fight, you want to fight effectively. You want to use your head. You want to keep your cool. And part of this is, I think, essentially joviality.

Joe Rigney's talk yesterday was wonderful, and he pinpointed King Lune as the quintessential jolly man. He's king of Archenland. But he's the quintessential jovial character. He's not a pacifist. He's first in and last out. He is the fighting king, but he's the kind of fighting king that I would want to follow. There are people who are so hard-bitten—they're so disillusioned—that they're not going to motivate anybody to do anything. So that's in a nutshell what I would say.

Philip Ryken: Joviality is not the only mood of the Christian life, but somebody that does not have a godly, sanctified joviality perhaps has a one-dimensional or not as fully human expression of the Christian life. The New Testament seems to present both fasting and feasting as normative for the Christian experience—both lamentation and celebration. Most of us find it hard to get the balance or proportion right, but those are both strongly held values in the Gospels. And C. S. Lewis is one of the best exemplars we can think of as the jovial Christian.

Douglas Wilson: Yeah. The apostle Paul says in Corinthians, "We are sorrowful yet always rejoicing." So you can go through afflictions. There's tears and bruises and hard times, and that's what I think a biblical joviality means. Death is swallowed up by victory at the end, and we must never forget that.

John Piper: It seems to me that there are two ways to talk about how the groaning and grieving and weeping fit together with the rejoicing. One is to say they're always simultaneous. That's 2 Corinthians 6:10. "Sorrowful yet always rejoicing." In other words, they're coextensive. It's not sequential, like you're happy on Sunday and then sad on Monday because you just saw somebody who's starving on Monday and didn't think about him on Sunday. That's not what that verse means. However, in the next chapter Paul says, "I'm thankful that I grieved you but not because it was an end in itself but because you were grieved unto repenting, which leads to life and no regret" [see 2 Cor. 7:8–11]. Now there is something sequential about that. Or consider James 4:8–9, "Weep and wail, you sinners. Cleanse your hearts, you double-minded." He means get it done. Finish it, and then have a party. So there's two ways that are tough. They're both tough. One is simultaneous happiness all the time in tears, and the other is getting the sequence and proportionality of the rhythm of feasting and fasting, weeping and rejoicing rightly. I find personally both of those very difficult. I almost never am satisfied that I got it right. There's so many hurting people, and there's so many reasons to be happy that it's hard to nail that proportion for my family, for myself, for my church, and for my friends. So I'm just welcoming you to get in step with the Holy Spirit. We know that he can be grieved *and* that he is the Spirit whose second fruit is joy.

Douglas Wilson: If you have a true community of believers, if you are plugged into a church and are a vibrant member of that church and you take the words of the Scripture seriously, "Weep with those who weep; rejoice with those who rejoice," then you find yourself having to do a lot of those things in quick succession. You've got the funeral on Wednesday and the wedding on Friday or the funeral on Wednesday and the wedding rehearsal Thursday evening and then the wedding on Friday. And you've got to go from one to the other. We're not called to schizophrenic scatteredness. We are called to weep with those who weep and rejoice with those who rejoice. The thing I must have to orient me in all of this is the recognition at all times that this is a comedy, not a tragedy. This ends well. It is comedy not in the sense of a sitcom, but comedy in the sense of *The Divine Comedy*, where it ends well. So it begins with a garden. The Bible begins with a garden and ends with a garden city. It ends with the bride coming down the aisle. That's how it ends. That's the story I'm in. So if I'm preaching the funeral of someone whose death just shocked the whole congregation, do I know where I am? Do I know what kind of book I'm in? This goes back to your point of knowing the genre. Do I know the genre of the history of the world? It's a comedy.

Randy Alcorn: Many of you have had this experience. Certainly when I've been doing memorial services, the therapy of laughter occurs as certain stories are told about the loved one who's departed and is now with the Lord, and you'll have tears just streaming down your face and then laughter—and it's not a superficial laughter. It's a laughter that is an overcoming laughter. It's a laughter that says we know a God of joy, a God who is eternally happy, and we'll be happy for all eternity, and we'll be with him and enjoying that happiness, and our loved one has gone on to be with him. That doesn't minimize our tears, but it does give a tone to the memorial service that's remarkable. There are times when laughter is louder at memorial services than in a normal context, and when it's done for those reasons it's Christ-centered laughter. I think it's very healthy.

Let's come back to likening. All five of you guys are writers who use likening in your writing—some more, some less. How intentional is the use of likening? And how much of it have you picked up through reading Lewis and others? How do you think through that as a writer?

John Piper: I don't think it matters whether you must work at it or whether it oozes, provided it doesn't sound like you work at it. A lot of bad writing is likening that's awkward and mechanical and wooden and doesn't work. The best remedy for that is to read a lot of good writers, and Lewis is hard to improve upon. The reason I moved from saying that I didn't want you to think of Lewis as a likener, in that he wrote novels but also ruthlessly logical essays with saturations of likening, is so that you would all apply that to yourselves. I hope that in conversations you'll be more given to likening, to putting into words in a little conversation you have over supper tonight that what you experienced earlier today was like this. That will be interesting, and it will be illuminating.

So my answer to the question, "How do you think about it?" is: Yes, think about it, and think about it long enough so that you take all the steps necessary so that you don't need to be artificial or wooden or mechanical about it but so it just kind of flows.

Douglas Wilson: Lewis says something, I think it's in a short essay about liturgy—one of you can correct me—but he's talking about learning the steps of liturgy. He compares it to learning how to dance. When you're first learning how to dance, you're not dancing with your beloved; you're counting. You know, one-two-three, one-two-three, one-two-three.

Philip Ryken: Or one-two-three-oops.

Douglas Wilson: Yeah, one-two-three-oops.

Philip Ryken: One-two-three-sorry.

Douglas Wilson: One-two-sorry. One-sorry.

John Piper: I've never had that experience.

Douglas Wilson: Lewis says that when you're first doing it, you're thinking about one thing, but you're deliberately doing it so that you may get it into your muscle memory, and then you can think about it. When you learn how to dance, you can think about the one you're dancing with and not have to worry about the math. He says liturgy is the same way. He says that he didn't much mind what liturgy the Church of England picked as long as they would pick one and keep it that way so that he could learn it and then think about God as he did the steps. Well, I would say it's the same sort of thing with metaphor and learning to write. If you're wanting to be a writer, you should be very intentional to ransack books and read dictionaries.

You should also be very intentional to write things down. But you should focus on that so that after the early stages it just becomes routine, and things just come to you unbidden. John Bunyan says a wonderful thing at the beginning of *Pilgrim's Progress*, I think in the poem. He said, "And as I pulled, it came," talking about inspiration. As I pulled, it came. You prime the pump and get to a certain point where it just starts happening. You've learned how to do it. So I invest at the front end what I would say.

Kevin Vanhoozer: I've written a whole book on likening—seeing the Christian life as a drama. I began to pull at that, and it just kept coming and coming. And it didn't feel artificial. It felt organic, and I felt challenged, and I was caught up in my metaphor. There's a certain sense that we will know a good metaphor by its fruit, a good likening by its fruit, not just how many pages can you write, but what kind of impact on your life it is having. Is it drawing you into the gospel farther up and farther in?

Philip Ryken: We had a great example of that from Kevin today in his talk "Discipleship as Waking Up." I thought it was great when you came to the end of the transfiguration, and there were even details in the biblical text that were really coming to the fore because of this metaphoric world of waking up that you were presenting to us. We had a great example today of how effective it can be in communicating the gospel.

Kevin, you've written a lot on postmodernity. A couple of questions could be, "Has Lewis already said what he would say to postmodernity?" And, "If he came along seventy-five years later, what might he say today to our context?"

Kevin Vanhoozer: Well, we've already mentioned the negative critique. That's too Bulveristic. I want to say that again: Bulveristic. What would he see that's encouraging? He might see imagination. But as we've heard from John, it has been unhooked—unhooked from the horse that should be pulling it, which is a particular epistemology. In my paper I was trying to use the words *discipline* and *disciple* quite a bit. The imagination must not be undisciplined, and it must not be hooked to some other horse. You know, we've got to make sure that we're following the authoritative imagining that we have in Scripture. There's a book out there called *Metaphorical Theology*, and the author says, "I'm just doing what the Bible is doing. The Bible uses metaphors. I'm using metaphors." But in this case—it's a woman—she uses this idea of metaphorical theology to invent her own metaphors, so she is not disciplined by biblical images. Instead of seeing God as Father and Lord, she suggests that we see God as mother and comrade. Well, those images carry a host of associations, and some of them may be less helpful than others. But the point is that she doesn't recognize the authority of the biblical imagination. So I'm not sure that Lewis would be all that encouraged to see more people imagining if the imagination is not being disciplined with the authority of Scripture.

John Piper: So, practically, how do these folks do that phrase, "biblically disciplined imagination"? What's that? What do those first two words means for their daily life?

Kevin Vanhoozer: It means we need to exchange the metaphors of the stories we live by. We need to get rid of the worldly metaphors and stories we live by—stories about what it is to be a success, for example—and we need to try to learn what success looks like in biblical terms. Success in biblical terms isn't necessarily a matter of how many people recognized you or how much money you made. Success is about our faithful witness to Jesus. This might be a matter of becoming poor for his sake—of giving up everything. That doesn't look like wisdom when you have certain metaphors and stories that the world tells us. So we have to deprogram ourselves.

John Piper: And the means of doing that, I would presume, is marinating your brain in the Bible.

Kevin Vanhoozer: If you steep yourself in Scripture, first of all, a lot of the false masks will come off. I think there's a moment of deprogramming. Just as Genesis 1 tells the true story of the creation, it also reveals other stories as myths to some extent. There's a certain demythologizing that goes on in Genesis. But if we accept the biblical story as the true story, it will challenge other stories we've been living by. Marination is a good idea.

Douglas Wilson: One thing I would add is that we must be steeped in Scripture. Charles Spurgeon once said of John Bunyan that if you pricked him anywhere, his blood would run bibline. He would bleed Bible verses. But we can't just bleed Bible verses or bleed doctrines. We have to bleed narratival structures. We have to bleed the exile in return, death, and resurrection. We have to bleed the structure or the story arc. That's part of what we have to be steeped in. There's a great chapter in a great book by Chesterton. The book is *Orthodoxy*, and the chapter is "The Ethics of Elfland." There, he shows how fairy stories are all biblically structured narratives. So I'll just make up one on the spot.

Once upon a time, there was a little boy named Tommy, and he lived in a green castle on the edge of the sea. And his fairy godmother came to him one day and said, "Under no circumstances are you to go into the north tower."

Now, you all know what's going to happen. Tommy's going to go into the north tower. Something really bad is going to happen as a consequence. And there's going to be an opportunity for redemption, and everything's going to be put right somehow at the cost of a great sacrifice on someone's part. How do we know that? We'll that's the garden of Eden. That's the history of the world. The history of Tommy is Everyman. Tommy is Adam. And we should recognize that kind of structure instantly. Fairy stories do that. Folk stories do that. In our modern world we try to mess with the structure, and we're impudent and disobedient and running away from the Bible.

Randy Alcorn: One of the things about story that comes to my mind, as it sort of connects to what we've been talking about, is the modern emphasis. I think Lewis would say there's good in this. People are talking about story and how our lives are stories and how we are to live out our story the way it was intended to be lived. But there's a huge downside to that. I see many believers now kind of celebrating *my* story—the story of *my* life. It's like we're becoming the stars of our teeny, little stories. It's *my* story. It's about *me*, and there's a whole bunch of them. Instead, we should see God's expansive story in which I am to be a role player in a small part in his great story, which is so much better than being the star of some pitiful, miserable little story that's all about me. I think that's one of the things that Lewis would see through right away with some of the discussion about telling our stories. Fine. Let's tell our stories. Let's talk about what God has done in our lives and how he may intend for me to live out my little place in his big story.

Douglas Wilson: One of the ways you can tell if people are doing the "me story" thing is if they are constantly plugged into their iPhone with ear buds so they can have a soundtrack. They're walking down the street with the soundtrack going, glancing at semi-mirrors of the storefront windows and watching themselves in their movie.

John Piper: What if they're listening to Doug Wilson?

Douglas Wilson: Then they're seriously screwed up.

A final question. Maybe for those here who haven't yet spent much time with Lewis or for a younger generation, loving Lewis wouldn't just be an evangelical Boomer phenomenon, but Millennials would love him too. If you're going to boil it down and say one thing to a younger generation, to those who don't know Lewis yet, why? Why spend time with him? Why be influenced and shaped by Lewis?

Randy Alcorn: Well, Lewis said that George MacDonald baptized his imagination. God used C. S. Lewis to baptize my imagination in a way that George MacDonald never could. And I think with Lewis, some of the people whom he so admired and drew from, I read them and I think, "This is fine." But Lewis is the one whom God has used in the lives of so many people. You think of the number of people just in terms of quantity. Chuck Colson, who is with the Lord now, for many years would talk about how God used *Mere Christianity* in his life. If you poll a large number of people and ask, "What books have had a huge impact on your life?" *Mere Christianity* is going to come up toward the top on almost every one of those lists. And then you'll get Narnia, and sometimes you'll get more obscure things of Lewis. His space trilogy had a tremendous impact on me. I would say just by sheer numbers of people who have gone before you, your chances of being highly influenced for the good through C. S. Lewis are very high.

Douglas Wilson: Lewis said somewhere about Edmund Spenser's *Faerie Queene* that to read Spenser is an exercise in mental health. I would say the same thing about reading Lewis. He is a bracing dose of sanity in a world gone mad. I think we need that kind of engaged touchstone. I think he's just wonderful. And if I might, I'd like to say—if you've never read Lewis—I would just encourage you to start simple with something like *The Screwtape Letters*. It's very accessible and just straight in. I'd like to mention that my favorite Lewis book is probably *That Hideous Strength*. I think it's one of the great novels of the twentieth century, and it's just glorious.

Philip Ryken: Maybe taking my cue from the talk last night—romantic, rationalist, likener, evangelist—and seeing it a slightly different way, Lewis shows us a person whose heart and head were both completely captive to Jesus Christ, combined in one person who could see from what was in this world the things that were pointing us to another world in ways that led him to want to share so that people would understand the gospel. I think there are a lot of people who would love to be a whole person—heart and head—for Jesus Christ, taking what's in the world and seeing what's missing in the world, pointing people to another world. C. S. Lewis can help you do that as well as anybody I know.

John Piper: If the misgiving of a millennial is that he appeals to baby boomers, the answer is, he was already totally out of date in the 1930s. Therefore he's no more out of date today than he was then. Since he was out of date in the 1930s, he is perpetually relevant. You don't need any more cool, hip, relevant people. You need somebody with roots who is so bright intellectually and so creative imaginatively that he communicates to your deepest needs. I would just piggyback on your piggybacking on me and say you are all romantics, and you're all rationalists. You are made in the image of a God who is joyful, and you're made in the image of a God who is rational. And Lewis will, by being so healthy in both of those, awaken the best in you. Whether you're twenty-five or sixty-five, we want that. It feels wonderful to have our romantic and rational sides made whole—made healthy by having somebody talk to us out of the context of such remarkable mental health.

Douglas Wilson: Speaking of relevance, Lewis once said, "Whatever's not eternal is eternally out of date."

Would you close us in prayer, John?

John Piper: Let's pray. Father, we've said it already and we'll say it again, that we are gathered here to see you and the path of discipleship with Jesus, crucified and risen, through the lens of your servant C. S. Lewis. So increase the clarity of that lens for us now. And may the entirety of our time together awaken affections that may have died or may have never existed, and sharpen thinking that may have grown dull so that we come alive to what you've made us to be and can be better representatives of you in our creative language and our articulate doctrine. I commend these brothers and sisters to you now, in Jesus's name. Amen.

ACKNOWLEDGMENTS

Well did Lewis capture the camaraderie of Christian Hedonism we feel in the mission of desiringGod.org. In his chapter on friendship in *The Four Loves*, he gives us the image of partnership "side by side, absorbed in some common interest."[1] True friendship is built on some specific and significant shared mission. And so, "friends hardly ever [talk] about their Friendship,"[2] but rather some great object—some great truth they see together, and about which they greatly care. We may picture Lovers face-to-face looking into each other's eyes, but we envision Friends side by side, eyes looking ahead.

God has been kind to us in giving the team at desiringGod.org not just companions in the mission, but real friendships. Along with the executive leadership—Jon Bloom, Scott Anderson, and Josh Etter—there is an unusual *esprit de corps* among the content team with whom I labor week in and week out. I thank God for Stefan Green, Jonathan Parnell, Tony Reinke, and Marshall Segal with whom we daily press on in biblicity and devotionality and creativity and gospel centrality and the pursuit of joy. Along with the writing of John (Piper) and Jon (Bloom), and the leadership of Scott and Josh, it takes the serious, full-throttle, ready-to-inject-humor engagement of this team to make our daily content offerings at desiringGod.org be what they are.

This volume is now the eleventh and final Desiring God National Conference book. The first conference was held at the three hundredth anniversary of the birth of Jonathan Edwards, in October of 2003, and the first volume (*A God-Entranced Vision of All Things*) appeared the

---

[1] C. S. Lewis, *The Four Loves* (New York: Harcourt, 1960), 61.
[2] Ibid.

following year, in partnership with Crossway. Working with Piper, Justin Taylor shepherded the first six books to press, and now I've had the privilege of stewarding these last five. Under God, without the on-the-ground energy and investment of Scott, with Dave Clifford, there would have been no Desiring God National Conferences. And without Justin and our ministry partners at Crossway—Lane Dennis, Al Fisher, Lydia Brownback, and more—we would not have this set of what we hope is eleven enduring resources for the church.

C. S. Lewis is a fitting conclusion to this series of eleven. The two writer-thinkers who have most shaped John's life and ministry, and this strand of theology we like to call "Christian Hedonistic," are Edwards and Lewis. The first volume celebrated Edwards; now this last one, Lewis. Along the way, we remembered John Calvin (2010), and we tackled the topics of sex (2005), suffering (2006), postmodernism (2007), perseverance (2008), the power of words (2009), the life of the mind (2011), global missions (2012), and Christian sanctification (2013).

But now, in this season ahead, we hope to dig and solidify the foundation beneath, and the strength in, these important areas of focus. For John and the team here at desiringGod.org, our life-after-the-National-Conference is a new venture we're calling "Look at the Book." It's a fresh effort to help Christians new and old go deeper in reading the Bible for themselves. John wrote this recently in announcing our new season:

> So I have a new and focused passion to help people really see the riches of God's word for themselves, and that has new and exciting implications for me and for the ministry of Desiring God.
>
> When I think of the coming generations, I am not content to only leave them a deposit of books and sermons that celebrate the glories of God and the wonders of Christian Hedonism. . . . If future generations only learn what we saw, and not how to see it for themselves, they will be second-handers. And second-handers cannot last. They grow bored and boring. Powerful, truth-pre-

serving, God-glorifying, Christ-exalting, soul-ravishing, mission-advancing ministry is sustained by the power to see for yourself the glories of God's word.

Our hope is that the caterpillar of our National Conference—and he's been a wonderfully fruitful caterpillar—will become this butterfly called "Look at the Book," which will help Christians dig ever deeper in God's own words and bring greater ballast to our lives in these stormy, increasingly post-Christian days for the Western church.

All this, of course, is our little endeavor, we hope empowered by the Spirit, for the glory of our Lord, Savior, and Treasure, Jesus Christ. It has been our aim, in all things Internet, and all things conferencing and publishing, to make much of him by presenting glimpses into the grandeur of who he is and readying Christians to live for his fame with ever-ripening satisfaction in him. Above and beneath and in all our gratitude for our friends at desiringGod.org and ministry partners at Crossway, we acknowledge and adore Jesus. It all is empty apart from him, and all future ventures to help people read their Bibles, or whatever else, are vain, unless his blessing is on it. Knowing him and enjoying him is the great goal of our lives and every ministry effort.

David Mathis
Minneapolis, Minnesota
May 5, 2014

GENERAL INDEX

SCRIPTURE INDEX

✳ desiringGod

Everyone wants to be happy. www.desiringGod.org was born and built for happiness. We want people everywhere to understand and embrace the truth that *God is most glorified in us when we are most satisfied in him*. We've collected more than thirty years of John Piper's speaking and writing, including translations into more than 40 languages. We also provide a daily stream of new written, audio, and video resources to help you find truth, purpose, and satisfaction that never end. And it's all available free of charge, thanks to the generosity of people who've been blessed by the ministry.

If you want more resources for true happiness, or if you want to learn more about our work at Desiring God, we invite you to visit us at www.desiringGod.org.

www.desiringGod.org